Dear Friend of the Radio Bible Class:

Please accept this volume on Galatians as an expression of our appreciation for your past interest and help in keeping the broadcast of the Class on the air, sending the Gospel message to the ends of the earth.

M R DeHaan

Galatians 6:14

GALATIANS

GALATIANS

Twenty-two Simple Studies in Paul's Teaching
of Law and Grace

by
M. R. DE HAAN, M.D.

RADIO BIBLE CLASS
Grand Rapids, Mich.

Printed in the United States of America

DEDICATION

To the memory of that dear saint of God, and able Bible Teacher, William L. Pettingill, who first introduced me to the blessed truth of grace and freedom from the law,

THIS VOLUME IS GRATEFULLY DEDICATED

THE AUTHOR

FOREWORD

The messages in this volume were prepared originally for radio broadcasting. They were delivered over the two coast-to-coast networks of the Mutual Broadcasting System and the American Broadcasting Company. They are reproduced in this volume almost word for word as they were given over the air, with a minimum of editing. For this reason there is some repetition and frequent reviewing of earlier material. This repetition was intentional and is done to emphasize the main theme of the Epistle and the more important passages.

I wish to express my gratitude to God for sending into my life, early in my ministry, one man who is now in Glory, and who was used to open my eyes to the grace of God in its fullness, and set me free from the yoke of bondage of the law. Coming from a background of legalism and sabbatarianism, it was not easy to repudiate some of my earlier convictions and accept without reservation the revelation of God concerning the believer's relation as "dead to the law" (Gal. 2:19), "loosed from the law" (Rom. 7:2), "delivered from the law" (Rom. 7:6), and "free from the law" (Rom. 8:2). God's instrument to lead me into this glorious truth was the late Dr. William L. Pettingill. This precious saint of God, now in Heaven, first made clear to me the glorious truth of the pure grace of God, early in my ministry as he spoke for one week on the Book of Galatians. At first he alarmed me, then he surprised me, then he shocked me, and then convinced me. To the memory of my spiritual teacher in the grace of God, beloved Dr. William Pettingill, I would dedicate this volume.

M. R. De Haan, M.D.

INTRODUCTION

The relation between Law and Grace in the plan of salvation has been a burning question since apostolic days. The transition from the age of Law which ended at Calvary, to the dispensation of Grace was not a sudden change without incident, but a bitter struggle. It was not easy for the believing Jew, brought up under the law of commandments and ordinances, to accept without question the new message of Grace, not fully revealed or made known before Pentecost. To reconcile the "Gospel of the Kingdom," as preached by the apostles in Matthew 10, and Acts 2, with the Gospel of the Grace of God as preached by Paul, was not an easy matter. The Apostle Paul had received his commission directly from God (Gal. 1:1; Gal. 2:1-9). It was the message of the grace of God, salvation by faith, wholly apart from the works of the law. The Jews who were God's chosen peculiar people, considered the Gentiles as dogs. The only way these Gentiles could be saved was by becoming Jewish proselytes, by being circumcised and submitting themselves to the Law of Moses. When, therefore, Paul preached salvation to the Gentiles, he met with violent opposition from these legalists. Paul had taught that men were saved just by "believing" the Gospel, wholly apart from the rite of circumcision and the works of the Law.

But the Jews in Judaea refused to accept this new message, and followed Paul wherever he went, seeking to discredit his message, and teaching instead that a man must be saved by ritual and legalism. They said, "Except ye be circumcised after the manner of Moses, ye cannot be saved" (Acts 15:1).

So fierce was the argument that it was thrashed out in the council at Jerusalem in Acts 15. Here it was decided that the Gentiles did NOT have to be circumcised, and did NOT have to be placed under the Law of Moses TO BE SAVED. Peter sums it up in Acts 15:7-11. The charge by the legalistic sect (Acts 15:5) was "that it was needful to circumcise them (the Gentiles), and to command them to keep the law of Moses." The decision of the council was clear, as stated in the letter sent to the Gentile churches:

> Forasmuch as we have heard, that certain which went out from us have troubled you with words, subverting your souls, saying, YE MUST BE CIRCUMCISED, AND KEEP THE LAW: TO WHOM WE GAVE NO SUCH COMMANDMENT (Acts 15:24).

The decision can be summed up in the words of Acts 15:11,

> But we believe that through the grace of the Lord Jesus Christ we shall be saved, even as they.

Salvation by grace, wholly apart from the works of the Law, was for all, the Jews as well as the Gentiles. This being settled, the legalists, refusing to admit their error, attacked the Gospel from another angle. It having been settled that the believer is saved by Grace, without being circumcised and keeping the Law, they now began to teach that while we are saved by Grace, WE MUST BE KEPT BY THE LAW, INCLUDING CIRCUMCISION. Instead of a requirement BEFORE salvation, circumcision is now proposed by the Judaists as a SUPPLEMENT TO FAITH for full fellowship and ultimate salvation. Paul's Galatian converts, these Judaizers admit, had "begun in the Spirit" but now they must endure to the end by the works of the law, even to the point of being circumcised (Gal. 3:3-5).

This was the teaching which these legalistic Judaizers had brought to the Galatian churches, after Paul had preached salvation by grace—plus nothing. It caused no end of confusion, and in response to the news of their defection from his teaching of grace, the Epistle to the Galatians was written. In the days of Paul there were three errors concerning Law and Grace, errors which have continued until this day, although the truth is so clearly taught in the Scriptures. These errors are:

1. LEGALISM. It is the teaching that we are saved by works, by observing rituals and ceremonies, and keeping the Law. One entire book of the New Testament is devoted to an answer to this soul-damning error. It is the Epistle to the Romans, summed up in Romans 3:28,

> Therefore we conclude that a man is justified by faith WITHOUT THE DEEDS OF THE LAW.

2. The second error is ANTI-NOMIANISM. It teaches that because we are saved by grace it makes no difference how we live and behave. One book of the New Testament is devoted to answering this Satanic error. It is the Book of James, summed up in James 2:17,

> Even so faith, if it hath not works, is dead, being alone.

3. GALATIANISM. This is the false doctrine which teaches that we are saved by grace, and then after that we are KEPT by the Law, making our ultimate salvation dependent on OUR WORKS instead of the GRACE OF GOD. To combat this error the Holy Spirit chose Paul to write the Epistle to the Galatians. It is the strongest argument that we are SAVED, KEPT, AND FINALLY REDEEMED BY GRACE, without the works of the law.

The problem in Galatia was, that having "begun in the Spirit," they now sought to be perfected by the flesh (Gal. 3:3). To the teaching that the believer, after he is saved by grace, is kept saved only by keeping the Law, Paul gives this testimony:

> For I through the law am dead to the law, that I might live unto God (Gal. 2:19).

The seriousness of claiming works in salvation may be seen from the curse pronounced upon these false teachers (Gal. 1:7-9) and by the terrible charge that their false gospel frustrates the grace of God, and accuses God of needlessly sacrificing His Son Jesus Christ.

This Epistle to the Galatians was written to Gentiles in Galatia who had believed the Gospel. But the message is as much needed, and even more, in these days of a mongrel gospel of grace and law. Galatianism is the subtlest of all the errors concerning the place of law-works in salvation. We send this volume forth with a prayer that it may set men free. Our prayer is that sinners may see that salvation is by FAITH, and not by works. For the believers we pray this volume may help them to:

> Stand fast therefore in the liberty wherewith Christ hath made us free, and be not entangled again with the yoke of bondage (Gal. 5:1).

We may well gather up the message of Galatians as follows:

Salvation is not a matter of LAW *and* GRACE, but it is a matter of LAW *or* GRACE, for it cannot be both. Read Romans 11:6.

M. R. DE HAAN

CONTENTS

GALATIANS

Chapter One

THE NEW MESSAGE OF GRACE

> Paul, an apostle, (not of men, neither by man, but by Jesus Christ, and God the Father, who raised him from the dead;)
>
> And all the brethren which are with me, unto the churches of Galatia (Gal. 1:1, 2).

THERE are 27 books in the New Testament. Of these 27 books, over half were written by one man—the Apostle Paul. If we accept the Pauline authorship of Hebrews, then 14 out of the 27 New Testament books were written by Paul. He is the outstanding apostle of the New Testament. His letters contain revelation found nowhere else in the Bible, and but for the letters of Paul, we would be in almost total darkness concerning the truth of the Church as the Body of Christ, its function, activity and destiny. His message was a new message, a mystery not known before—a message received direct from Heaven as a new revelation of divine truth. The heart of this new message was the "grace of God," extended to all men everywhere, wholly and entirely apart from the works of the law. The message before this had been limited to the Nation of Israel, and the Gentiles could only be saved by becoming Jews, submitting to the rite of circumcision and placing themselves under the laws and rituals of the Israelites. These are called Jewish proselytes.

THE MAN PAUL

When Paul came with his message of grace, it met with
serious misgivings by the eleven apostles, who were still
preaching the Kingdom message to the Jews only. Because of his prominence in the New Testament we now
mention some things about Paul personally, which will
help us to understand this opposition and rejection by
the Judaizers. Paul was a Jew—born in Tarsus, a son of
a Roman citizen. He received his secular education in
Tarsus, and his theological training in Jerusalem under
the great teacher, Gamaliel (Acts 22:3). He was a member of the Sanhedrin, the highest ruling religious body
in Israel, a prominent member of the strictest sect of
the Pharisees. He was devoted to Judaism, and was fa-
natical in his defense of what he believed to be the only
true religion. He took a prominent part in the martyr-
dom of Stephen, and became a bitter enemy of Chris-
tianity. While on a mission to arrest and prosecute the
Christians in Damascus, he was dramatically converted
by a personal meeting with the Lord Jesus. Smitten with
blindness for three days, he was befriended by one of the
despised believers in Damascus, Ananias, who entertained
and baptized him, and Paul launched out on his ministry.

HIS PREPARATION

After Paul's conversion, he made a brief visit to Jerusalem, but the Christians there were afraid of him, and
he soon left and departed for his home city of Tarsus,
and from there went to Arabia for three years, where he
received the revelation of the new message of the mystery
of the Church, the Body of Christ, and the Age of Grace.
It was undoubtedly when here in Arabia, that he was
caught up into Heaven and heard and saw the things
recorded in II Corinthians 12. After three years he re-

turns to Tarsus where he is found by Barnabas and brought to Antioch. Here they labored for one whole year and saw great numbers of the Gentiles brought to Christ.

First Missionary Journey

After this year of ministry in Antioch, Paul and Barnabas made a brief trip to Jerusalem to bring relief to the poor suffering Jewish disciples, and upon their return to Antioch are sent forth as the first Christian missionaries. The balance of the Book of Acts deals almost exclusively with the journeys and ministry of the Apostle Paul. After his first missionary journey, Paul is called to give a report, and to account for his message before the apostles in Jerusalem (Acts 15). His enemies accused him of preaching heresy and he went to Jerusalem to report before the apostles. Here it was decided that the message of the grace which Paul preached to the Gentiles was truly the message of Christ from Heaven. It was decided that the Gentile Christians were not under the Jewish law. This is the last time the apostles in Jerusalem are mentioned. Peter and all the rest of the eleven with their Kingdom message to Israel, now bow out of the picture, Israel is temporarily set aside, the Kingdom is postponed, and the new message of grace brought by Paul now goes to the entire world.

It is well to note here the sharp and distinct difference between the message Paul preached and the message committed to the apostles. The message of Peter was to Israel, while Paul is the Apostle to the Gentiles. This was also agreed upon. In Galatians 2:7 we read:

> . . . when they saw that the gospel of the uncircumcision was committed unto me, as the gospel of the circumcision was unto Peter;

> . . . they gave to me and Barnabas the right hands of fellow-
> ship; that we should go unto the heathen (Gentiles), and
> they unto the circumcision (Gal. 2:7, 9).

The apostles never went to any but Jews with their
Kingdom message. On only one occasion did an apostle
go to the Gentiles. This was when Peter preached to
a Gentile (Cornelius, Acts 10), to exercise the final use
of the keys. The apostles established no churches outside
of Judaea, but limited their ministry to Jerusalem and
the Jews. Even after the death of Stephen when the
Church was scattered, the apostles continued in Jerusalem ministering only to Israel. After Stephen's death
we read:

> . . . they were all scattered abroad throughout the regions
> of Judaea and Samaria, EXCEPT THE APOSTLES (Acts
> 8:1).

Even those who were scattered abroad, did not preach
to the Gentiles. We read concerning these:

> Now they which were scattered abroad . . . travelled as far
> as Phenice, and Cyprus, and Antioch, preaching the word
> to none but unto THE JEWS ONLY (Acts 11:19).

When some of them did begin to preach to the Grecians
(Grecian Jews) the apostles sent Barnabas to investigate
(Acts 11:22). But when Barnabas saw the grace of God
among these Grecians he did not go back to report to
the apostles, who had sent him, but instead went immediately to Tarsus to find Paul, and brought him back
to Antioch. Barnabas knew the apostolic message was
not for Antioch, but that Paul was the man to take over
with the new message of grace.

The eleven apostles never founded any Gentile
churches. It was Paul who was God's messenger for this
dispensation. As a result of Paul's ministry, Gentile as-

semblies resulted in Antioch, Corinth, Galatia, Thessalonica, Ephesus, Philippi, Colosse, and others. Unless we keep this background in mind, that Paul's distinctive message was to all men, Jews and Gentiles, we cannot rightly divide the Word of Truth and reconcile the Gospel which Paul preached with the message of the apostles. It will also explain the bitter opposition Paul experienced from his brethren according to the flesh. They had been taught to consider Gentiles as unclean dogs and outside the covenant of grace. When Paul therefore offered to these Gentiles salvation by grace alone, they were most bitter in their opposition and finally succeeded in bringing about his arrest and execution. It will also explain why Paul was always and everywhere called upon to defend his apostleship. They would not accept him as an apostle because he did not receive his commission from the apostles, nor did he preach the apostolic message.

THE MESSAGE

Before closing this introductory message, we wish to show the difference between the Kingdom message given to the twelve apostles and preached by them, and the grace message as committed to Paul. The Kingdom message preached by John the Baptist and the apostles is summed up in Matthew 10. This message was only for the apostles and only to Israel. We read:

> And when he had called unto him his twelve disciples, he gave them power against unclean spirits, to cast them out, and to heal all manner of sickness and all manner of disease (Matt. 10:1).

To apply this verse today as the authority for casting out demons and promiscuous healing is to wrest the Scriptures. One must first prove that he is one of the

twelve apostles before these powers can be claimed. And
to make it foolproof, the twelve apostles are then enu-
merated by name.

Notice next the command to limit their ministry. The
words are unmistakable:

> These twelve Jesus sent forth, and commanded them, say-
> ing, Go not into the way of the Gentiles, and into any city
> of the Samaritans enter ye not:
> But go rather to the lost sheep of the house of Israel (Matt.
> 10:5, 6).

The Kingdom message was not the message for the
Church, but for Israel alone.

Then notice the message. It is "the Kingdom of heaven
is at hand." It was the offer of the setting up of the
Messianic Kingdom upon condition of national repentance. This is not the message Paul preached. His message was, "Believe on the Lord Jesus Christ, and thou
shalt be saved" (Acts 16:31). And then follow the signs
of the Kingdom. The evidence of the Kingdom message
were signs and wonders.

> Heal the sick, cleanse the lepers, raise the dead, cast out
> devils: freely ye have received, freely give (Matt. 10:8).

To use this verse as authority for divine healing is to
utterly ignore the simplest rule of reason and logic.
These apostles not only healed the sick, but RAISED
THE DEAD, AND CLEANSED THE LEPERS.

Next notice the support of these ministers. They were
to take no offerings:

> Provide neither gold, nor silver, nor brass in your purses,
> Nor scrip for your journey, neither two coats, neither
> shoes, nor yet staves: for the workman is worthy of his
> meat (Matt. 10:9, 10).

These evangelists with the Kingdom message were

to depend wholly upon charity. Compare this to the methods of some who quote from this chapter as authority for their unscriptural procedures. Read the rest of the chapter and see how it completely conflicts with the modern methods of those who claim these apostolic gifts.

PAUL'S MESSAGE

This then was the apostolic message of the Kingdom. But what a contrast we find when Paul begins his ministry after the apostolic program is interrupted temporarily until the Church Age is completed and this dispensation ends. Failure to distinguish between the Kingdom message given by Christ to the apostles, and the new message of grace given by Christ to Paul and the disciples, AFTER the rejection by Israel of the Kingdom offer, is at the root of all the confusion among Christians. Unless we recognize God's dispensational dealings we cannot understand the Bible, but it will appear to be full of contradictions. To apply the Kingdom message to the Church, and to mix law and grace results in confusion, chaos, fanaticism, error and misunderstanding. For instance, how can we reconcile God's command in the Old Testament to Israel to destroy their enemies, slay men, women and children, burn their cities and appropriate their wealth, with the New Testament message of grace which commands us to preach salvation to all the world?

How can we reconcile Jesus' words to the apostles, "Go not into the way of the Gentiles—go only to the house of Israel" (Matt. 10), with the message of Romans 10:

> For there is no difference between the Jew and the Greek; for the same Lord over all is rich unto all that call upon him.

For whosoever shall call upon the name of the Lord shall be saved (Rom. 10:12, 13).

Did God change His mind? Why did God command the adulterers and adulteresses to be put to death under the Old Testament dispensation of the Law, while Christ dealt in mercy with one taken in the very act? The Law commands a rebellious son to be stoned (Deut. 21:18-21) but Grace received the prodigal in love (Luke 15:11-25). A thief was condemned under the law (Ex. 21:16), but the thief on the Cross was forgiven. The Law says, "Eye for eye, tooth for tooth, hand for hand, foot for foot" (Ex. 21:24). But Grace says, "If thine enemy hunger, feed him; if he thirst, give him drink" (Rom. 12:20). It is impossible to reconcile such passages, unless we recognize God's dispensational dealings under Law and under Grace. The law condemns the sinner—grace forgives.

It was failure to recognize the difference between the Kingdom message and the message of Grace, the distinction between Law and Grace, which caused the persecutions of the Apostle Paul, and which resulted in his execution. It is no different today. Failure to study the Bible dispensationally, is the cause of all the misunderstanding and division among Christians. Ninety percent of the difficulty would end if we would only recognize the totally different program of God for National Israel and for the Church. To apply the message for Israel to the Church can only lead to confusion. It is to correct this damaging error that Romans and Galatians were written.

And we pray that these messages on the Book of Galatians may remove the veil of legalism and cause many to have their eyes opened to the liberty of grace, and to not only be saved by grace, but TO LIVE BY GRACE! Then we shall see souls attracted to Christ by the grace of Christ in our lives.

Chapter Two

THE AUTHORITY OF PAUL

> Paul, an apostle, (not of men, neither by man, but by Jesus Christ, and God the Father, who raised him from the dead;) (Gal. 1:1).

THIRTEEN of the twenty-seven books of the New Testament begin with the same word, "Paul." If we accept the Pauline authorship of Hebrews, then fourteen of the twenty-seven books of the New Testament were written by Paul. Matthew wrote only one; Luke, two; John wrote five; Peter wrote two; and Jude and James only one each. The other apostles never left us any literature of any kind. Mark and Luke were not among the apostles, and received much of their information from the Apostle Paul. The Book of Acts was written by Luke, and over half of it is an account of Paul's experiences and travels. We may therefore call the Book of Acts a Pauline book, for seventeen of the twenty-eight chapters deal with the life of Paul, and from Acts 15 on, the other apostles are never mentioned. Their ministry to the Nation of Israel now disappears in the light of Paul's ministry to the Gentiles.

PAULINE BOOK

From these facts we are justified in calling the New Testament a Pauline book, since it deals predominantly with the ministry of this Apostle to the Gentiles. Because of his unique and different message, received by special revelation from Heaven, he was not readily received by the other apostles. He was vigorously opposed by the legalistic teachers of his day, who followed him from place to place, seeking to discredit Paul's authority and deny his message of grace. As a result Paul was called upon again and again to defend himself against his accusers, and to prove his divine authority. Several of his epistles open with a declaration of his authority. Romans opens with "Paul, a servant of Jesus Christ, called to be an apostle." First Corinthians opens with, "Paul, called to be an apostle of Jesus Christ through the will of God." Second Corinthians opens with, "Paul, an apostle of Jesus Christ by the will of God." Ephesians opens with the same assertion of his divine apostolic appointment. In Colossians 1:1 he makes the same claim for authority by the will of God. First Timothy opens with, "Paul, an apostle of Jesus Christ by the commandment of God." In Second Timothy he again repeats his apostolic authority, and in Titus he once more asserts his claim to being an apostle. Finally, notice how the Epistle to the Galatians opens:

> Paul, an apostle, (not of men, neither by man, but by Jesus Christ, and God the Father, who raised him from the dead (Gal. 1:1).

WHY THIS EMPHASIS?

We are led to ask the question: Why all this emphasis upon his apostleship. Why did Paul have to defend his authority as an apostle wherever he went? There are several reasons: First, Paul was not chosen by the apostolic band in Jerusalem. He received his appointment directly from Heaven. Secondly, Paul's message was not the apostolic Kingdom message held by the Church in Jerusalem. Thirdly, Paul's ministry was not exclusively for the Jews, but primarily to the Gentiles. For these and other reasons, Paul was opposed by the Judaizing legalists, and even the apostles at Jerusalem questioned his authority. They refused to accept Paul as an apostle, for they had already taken care of the vacancy in the group of twelve resulting from the suicide of Judas. They had replaced Judas with Matthias (Acts 1:15-26). This was in direct violation of Jesus' instructions to them. Jesus had said to them to do NOTHING until AFTER the Holy Spirit had been poured out. It was a command. After His resurrection we read:

> And being assembled together with them, (he) commanded them that they should not depart from Jerusalem, but WAIT for the promise of the Father, which, saith he, ye have heard of me (Acts 1:4).

The apostles had strict orders to WAIT for the Holy Spirit before they did a single thing. They were to do NOTHING, for until the Spirit came, everything they did would be in the energy of the flesh. So Jesus said, "Don't do anything until the Spirit comes to guide and direct you." Until then everything they did would be wrong. Jesus promised power for service only after the Holy Spirit came. He had said:

> But ye shall receive power, AFTER that the Holy Ghost is come upon you (Acts 1:8).

Impatient Peter

But ten days seemed a long while to wait, and the apostles led by Peter became impatient. They wanted to get to work, and so they decided to get ready, so that when the Spirit came they could get busy. They knew the apostolic band was incomplete with only eleven apostles. Upon Peter's suggestion, therefore, they determined to elect a twelfth apostle to replace Judas. Instead of WAITING for the Holy Spirit to choose God's man, Peter suggested that they call a meeting, put up a slate of candidates and proceed to do the Holy Spirit's business. It is a sad story in Acts 1:15-26.

> And in those days (before the Holy Spirit came) Peter stood up. . . , and said, . . .
> Men and brethren . . .
> . . . of these men which have companied with us all the time that the Lord Jesus went in and out among us, . . . must one be ordained to be a witness with us of his resurrection (Acts 1:15, 16, 21, 22).

Where did Peter get this authority when Jesus had commanded, WAIT! Who told Peter the twelfth apostle had to be of that little company assembled there? Who gave them authority to ORDAIN an apostle? It was all in the energy of the flesh. They were not willing to wait for the Spirit to lead them, and so they went ahead.

> And they appointed two, Joseph called Barsabas, who was surnamed Justus, and Matthias (Acts 1:23).

The slate having been presented, they prayed the Lord to show which one was chosen. But their prayer was so much wasted breath, for they asked God to pick ONE of two candidates which THEY had chosen. Why didn't they pray for God to show them which two of the 120 were to be placed on the slate? This they took care of, but now limited God to His choice from these two, whom they had suggested. Would it not have been just as easy, and easier to ask the Lord to show His choice immediately, instead of waiting for a ticket with two names to be presented for the Lord? They did not permit God to vote for His choice, but limited Him to only two. They prayed, "shew which of these TWO." No wonder the Lord did not answer, and they were compelled to "cast lots" to determine the choice.

> And they gave forth their lots; and the lot fell upon Matthias; and he was numbered with the eleven apostles (Acts 1:26).

Casting lots, instead of waiting for the Spirit's direction! How different the appointment of the two first missionaries in Acts 13. There was no slate of candidates chosen by men, no shaking of dice, or putting names in a hat, but instead we read:

> As they ministered to the Lord, and fasted, the HOLY GHOST said, Separate me Barnabas and Saul for the work whereunto I have called them (Acts 13:2).

God's Choice—Paul

Evidently God never recognized the choice of Matthias, for he is never mentioned again in the rest of the Bible. God ignored man's ordination, and after the Holy Spirit came, He chose a man by the name of Paul to be an apostle. But it was not by man's choice, but an outright ordination by Christ. He was ordained for his office by God. He says in I Timothy 2:7 that he was "ordained a preacher, and an apostle, . . . a teacher of the Gentiles in faith and verity."

Paul Had No Credentials

For this reason Paul was not recognized as an official apostle. The company in Jerusalem held to the appointment of Matthias, and thus rejected Paul's claim to being an apostle. Everywhere he went he was trailed by the legalists who said, "Paul is not an apostle. He was never ordained by the elders in Jerusalem. He did not get his training from us. He is a counterfeit apostle, because he was not officially chosen by us, he was not licensed to preach by our denomination, he was not ordained by our ordination committee, and he isn't even a graduate of our seminary." This was the problem which confronted Paul everywhere and forced him constantly to defend his authority, his message and his method. Now you will understand why Paul opens so many of his epistles with a declaration of his authority. "Paul, an apostle of Jesus Christ by the will of God," he says. And in this introductory verse in Galatians 1, he declares:

Paul, an apostle.

Then he adds in parenthesis a devastating answer to his accusers who sought to deny his authority as an apostle. He says, I am an apostle but:

... (not of men, neither by man, but by Jesus Christ, and God the Father, who raised him from the dead;) (Gal. 1:1).

We shall see later where and when Paul received his divine commission. The first two chapters of Galatians, therefore, are occupied almost entirely with a defense of three things: (1.) His ministry; (2.) His method; and (3.) His message. These we shall take up in due time.

Before we close, just a word about the churches to which this Galatian epistle was written. It is unique, as it is the only letter written by Paul to a group of churches. All his other epistles were written either to individuals, such as Timothy, Philemon and Titus; or to individual churches (Rome, Corinth, Ephesus, Philippi, Colosse, and Thessalonica). But his letter to Galatia was an encyclical letter to be passed on to several churches in the region of Galatia in Asia Minor. On Paul's first missionary journey he had successfully preached in the cities of Antioch, Iconium, Derbe and Lystra. Here they had been gathered into local assemblies, ordained elders and left them happy in their new-found liberty of grace. But very soon false teachers came in who questioned Paul's authority as an apostle, and repudiated his message of grace, and taught these converts that they must be

circumcised, and keep the laws of Moses in order to be
saved. This was the occasion for Paul's letter to the
Galatian churches. It is Paul's answer to the false doctrine of the legalists, that we are saved by grace, and then
are kept by our works. The new message of Paul, received
from Heaven, but rejected by the legalistic Judaizers in
Jerusalem, was this: the Gentiles are saved by grace and
kept by grace, wholly apart from the works of the law.
The key word of the message of Paul was "grace," plus
nothing. The key passage of Galatians is Galatians 3:10-
12. The key verse of the book is Galatians 2:21,

> I do not frustrate the grace of God: for if righteousness
> come by the law, then Christ is dead in vain (Gal. 2:21).

The message of grace is salvation by faith in the Person
and finished work of Jesus Christ. It is simply believing
what the Bible says about Jesus Christ. It is not religion,
not good works, reformation, education, culture or ordinances. It is not ritual or ceremony, prayers or deeds of
charity. It is coming as a poor lost sinner, bankrupt and
helpless, and trusting Christ to save you by His grace.
Man would like to have just some little part in his own
salvation, but God says NO! You will never be able
to boast of your salvation, for salvation is of the Lord—
ALL of the Lord. Oh, sinner, let go—and let God.

Today the problem of the Galatians is still with us,
in spite of the clear teaching of the Word of God. Men
are made to believe they must DO something to be
saved. Man adds to salvation by grace, religion, good
works, church membership, ordinances, and the works of
the law. But the Bible says:

> But to him that worketh not, but believeth on him that
> justifieth the ungodly, his faith is counted for righteousness
> (Rom. 4:5).

Chapter Three

GRACE PLUS NOTHING

"GOOD things come in small packages," is a popular saying, which may or may not always be true. It is, however, true in the case of Paul's Epistle to the Galatians, which we are studying. It is not one of the longest epistles, containing only six comparatively brief chapters, but they are jammed full of most important doctrines and practical truths. No one can fully understand the relationship between Law and Grace, faith and works, Israel and the Church, without knowing the teaching of the grace of God as set forth in this and the Roman epistle. The letter was written by the Apostle Paul (verse 1). It was addressed to a group of churches in Galatia, a region in Asia Minor (verse 2). The theme of the letter is given in verse 3:

Grace be to you and peace.

The key word of the epistle is GRACE, and the fruit of grace is peace. In verse 4 we have the foundation for the grace of God extended to helpless sinners. This grace comes from God the Father and from our Lord Jesus Christ.

> Who gave himself for our sins, that he might deliver us from this present evil world, according to the will of God and our Father:
> To whom be glory for ever and ever. Amen (Gal. 1:4, 5).

Fullness of Grace

In these verses we have the following things said about the grace of God:

1. The channel of God's grace. It is Jesus Christ who gave Himself for our sins.

2. The purpose of God's grace. It is to deliver us from this present evil world.

3. The source of this grace. It is the sovereign will and purpose of God "according to the will of God and our Father."

4. Finally, we have the reason for God's grace. It is to bring glory only to God for ever and ever. Amen.

It is humanly impossible to adequately define the grace of God. Many attempts have been made, but all must fall short of fully describing it. Someone has said, "Grace is the unmerited favor of a holy God toward wholly sinful, ruined sinners." Another has said, "Grace is everything for nothing." While all this is true, it merely scratches the surface. Grace lifts the lowest sinner to the highest place in Heaven. But all of this is not because of anything in the sinner, but all of it surges from the heart of a loving God. Notice that grace excludes all human effort, works, righteousness or goodness. Grace is exclusively the work of God. Add so much as one grain of works, merit or human righteousness or effort, and it ceases to be grace.

Paul tells us we are saved by grace,

> . . . through faith; and that not of yourselves: it is the gift of God:
> Not of works, lest any man should boast.
> For we are HIS workmanship, created in Christ Jesus unto good works, which God hath before ordained that we should walk in them (Eph. 2:8-10).

Grace excludes all human effort. Salvation is all of the

Lord. Or listen to God's definition of grace in II Timothy
1:9. Speaking of the work of our Saviour, He says:

> Who hath saved us, and called us with an holy calling,
> not according to our works, but according to his own pur-
> pose and GRACE, which was given us in Christ Jesus before
> the world began (II Tim. 1:9).

Can you find any human effort or contribution in this
verse? It is all God's work. He saved us, He called us,
He purposed to save us by His grace, and He settled it
before we were born. He chose us before the foundation
of the world (Eph. 1:4), and this grace of salvation was
given us IN CHRIST JESUS before the world began.
He settled it all before we were born, so we wouldn't be
able to get our hands on it and ruin it all.

HANNAH'S DEFINITION

We emphasize this aspect of grace as being all of God,
because we cannot understand this epistle to the Galatians
without clearly recognizing the nature of grace. The
Galatian Christians were told by false legalistic teachers
that salvation was grace, "plus" works. They were saved
by grace—but then their ultimate salvation depended
upon their behavior, works, and keeping the law. This
error was the occasion for Paul writing this epistle—to
show that we are saved by grace—kept by grace—and will
be finally presented unblameable in His sight by grace.
To add even an infinitesimal speck of works to grace
spoils it all. Hannah, the mother of Samuel, gives a marvelous definition of grace in her prayer of thanksgiving
in I Samuel 2:6-8,

> The LORD killeth, and maketh alive: he bringeth down
> to the grave, and bringeth up.
> The LORD maketh poor, and maketh rich: he bringeth
> low, and lifteth up.

He raiseth up the poor out of the dust, and lifteth up the beggar from the dunghill, to set them among princes, and to make them inherit the throne of glory (I Sam. 2:6-8).

Search as you will in this definition of grace, and you will find nothing of man. It is all of God, from start to finish. He that begins the work of salvation also finishes it. Hannah says: It is all grace, it is all of God. He kills, He makes alive, He makes poor, He makes rich, He raises up the poor, He delivers the beggar from the dunghill, He it is who lifts him to the loftiest heights of glory, and makes the filthy, unworthy beggar an HEIR of the riches of Heaven. And having saved him, He also assures his security, for I Samuel 2:9 follows with the words:

He will keep the feet of his saints (I Sam. 2:9a).

I trust we have made it clear that salvation must be all of grace. The least bit of human help spoils it all. Listen once more to Paul in Romans 11:6, where he says that it is all according to God's sovereign election of grace:

And if by grace, then it is no more of works: otherwise grace is no more grace. But if it be of works, then is it no more grace: otherwise work is no more work.

Now returning to our Scripture notice how Paul expresses this truth of grace. He says (Gal. 1:3, 4):

Grace be to you and peace from God the Father, and from our Lord Jesus Christ,
WHO GAVE HIMSELF for our sins, that he might deliver us.

These words are inexhaustible. Of Jesus it is said He GAVE HIMSELF FOR OUR SINS. We are all familiar with the best-known verse in the Bible, where God gave His Son:

For God so loved the world, that he gave his only begotten Son, that whosoever believeth in him should not perish, but have everlasting life (John 3:16).

But here we read that Jesus gave HIMSELF. His sacrifice was voluntary. He offered Himself to die in the place of sinners. This verse does not say, "He gave Himself for sinners," but rather it says, "He gave Himself for our sins." Human words fail completely to convey the depth of the meaning of the expression, "He gave Himself for OUR SINS." It suggests a TRADE, an exchange. He offers us Himself, in exchange for our sins. He wants to save us. He loves the sinner so much that He will pay any price the Father demands. The price is the penalty of the law. God is a holy God and cannot condone sin. It must be put away before He can accept the sinner. But God is also a just God, and for sin to be put away, the penalty must be exacted. But the penalty was eternal death, eternal separation from God. Man could not pay it. It would take him an eternity in Hell to make satisfaction to a broken law.

And here the Saviour steps in. The law said the sinner is cursed, damned, condemned and must die the eternal death. But Christ offers to save that sinner. But the law must be satisfied before God can do so. A loving God cannot violate His justice. He cannot ignore His Word, "the soul that sinneth it shall die." How then can it be done? Jesus said, "I will take man's sin and make it my responsibility. I will bear its penalty, I will take the sinner's place." That is the meaning of our verse, He "gave Himself for our sins." When Jesus offered to take our place, God transferred to Him our sin. While we cannot understand this, the Scriptures are plain. Peter says that He,

> . . . bare our sins in his own body on the tree (I Pet. 2:24).

The Prophet Isaiah, writing hundreds of years before, says that:

> . . . he was wounded for our transgressions, he was bruised for our iniquities . . . (and that the)
> . . . Lord hath laid on him the iniquity of us all (Isa. 53:5, 6).

In order to redeem us from sin the Lord must take our sin and pay its penalty. But Paul in II Corinthians 5 goes still deeper and says:

> For he hath made him to be sin for us, who knew no sin (II Cor. 5:21).

What stupendous revelation is this! Christ became sin (not a sinner) for us. When Jesus took our sin upon Himself, God forsook Him, for God cannot look upon sin. When God looked upon Jesus He saw sin—our sin—and God condemned Jesus to die. God cursed Him. I realize it is difficult to believe that Jesus, when He took our place and became sin for us, became a cursed thing in God's sight which God had to turn away from. But that is the awful revelation of the Bible. He was made sin for us. In Galatians 3:13 Paul asserts:

> Christ hath redeemed us from the curse of the law, BE-ING MADE A CURSE for us: for it is written, CURSED is every one that hangeth on a tree (Gal. 3:13).

Yes, Jesus was made sin for us, and God hates sin, and turns from it. And now we come to the glorious consummation. It was in His BODY that Jesus bore our sin. The Spirit of Christ remained unaffected by sin. His soul also remained pure from our sin. When God laid our sin on Jesus it had to do only with His body . And because of that sin which He bare in His body, He must die the death. He must die physically. But an offering must be presented to atone for the sin He had taken upon Himself. He could not offer His body as an atonement, for in that body He bore our sin, and God cannot accept sin in payment for sin. Here indeed is a real problem.

The Bible gives the answer. Since the soul of Jesus was unaffected by our sin, He could therefore offer His sinless perfect soul as an offering for the sin He bare in His body. God demands an offering to take away sin. And that offering must satisfy the penalty of sin in full. And so Jesus offered to God His SOUL in payment for our sins, which He bore in His body on the tree. That is why His soul had to go to sheol; that is why He suffered the penalty for sin in His soul when He cried:

> My SOUL is exceeding sorrowful unto death (Mark 14:34).

He bare our sins in His body on the tree, but He presented His undefiled soul as the offering for our sins. This Isaiah asserts in Isaiah 53:10,

> Yet it pleased the LORD to bruise him; he hath put him to grief: when thou shalt make HIS SOUL an offering for sin, he shall see his seed (Isa. 53:10).

Yes, that too is the meaning of Galatians 1:4,

> Who gave HIMSELF for our sins.

This is the same as saying "He gave His soul." The soul is the real person. The body is but the temple for the soul—the medium of expression for the soul. The SOUL is the real YOU. When a person dies, the body only dies, the soul lives on. Jesus gave His body in death, but offered His soul (Himself) an offering for sin. And it was accepted and ratified by His resurrection from the dead. The resurrection is God's stamp of approval on the work of Christ, and His soul returned from sheol to enter His glorified, sinless body as the proof that NOT ONE SIN WAS LEFT UNPAID. It was finished.

And because it is finished, and He did it all, IT IS ALL OF GRACE. Nothing can be added to it. It must simply be accepted, for the Lord will not share His glory with another. Salvation is receiving this free gift by faith without any claim of our own, but **THE GRACE OF GOD.**

Chapter Four

GRACE—THE DEATH OF PRIDE

> I marvel that ye are so soon removed from him that called
> you into the GRACE of Christ unto another gospel:
> Which is not another; but there be some that trouble
> you, and would pervert the gospel of Christ (Gal. 1:6, 7).

THE central phrase of this passage is the "grace of
Christ." Paul expresses great surprise and frustration
of spirit at the fickleness of these Galatian believers who
had at first so joyfully accepted Paul's message of grace,
and then had been so easily led astray by certain legalistic
Judaizing teachers, who discredited Paul's teachings of
grace, and asserted that these believers were still under
the law, and were bound by the law of Moses. Paul
had preached that they were saved by grace—plus nothing.
There is nothing man can add to the grace of God, for
His whole salvation rests on the finished and completed
work of the Lord Jesus who "bare our sins in his own
body on the tree," and then gave His "soul an offering"
for those sins. Christ bore the curse of the law, being
made a curse for us, and now "Christ is the end of the
law to everyone that believeth."

Paul had left these Galatian believers happy and rejoicing and serving the Lord in the liberty of grace, not
by constraint of the law, not by fear of losing their salvation, but by love, gratitude and devotion for their great
salvation by grace. They loved Paul fervently and devotedly for showing them the truth of salvation by grace.

41

But then, as now, there were those who would enslave
the believer again, by the bondage of the law, and instead of trying to win sinners to Christ by grace, went
about proselyting Christians to their legalistic, false religion by claiming that, while we are saved by grace, we
are kept by works, and thus making our salvation dependent in the final analysis, not upon grace, but on
works and lawkeeping. These legalistic Judaistic law
teachers sought to bring the believers again under bondage and make them—

> . . . observe days, and months, and times, and years
> (Gal. 4:10).

They heeded not the warning of Paul in Colossians
2:16,

> Let no man therefore judge you in meat, or in drink,
> or in respect of an holyday, or of the new moon, or of the
> sabbath days:
> Which are a shadow of things to come; but the body is of
> Christ (Col. 2:16, 17).

But these Galatian Christians, still babes in Christ,
were carried away by the pious pratings of the false
teachers and their quoting of Scriptures out of their connection, deceived and beguiled by their clever preachers
of a mixed gospel of grace and law.

DISCREDITED PAUL

Naturally these false teachers discredited the teachings
of Paul, and placed him in a bad light. The inference was
that Paul had brought a false gospel—or at least an incomplete gospel. This affected their love for Paul, and they
lost respect for his authority. They now became en-
amored with these false teachers and their love for Paul
began to cool. This greatly grieved the apostle, and so
he writes:

> I marvel that ye are so soon removed from him (refer-
> ring to himself) that called you into the grace of Christ
> (Gal. 1:6).

The one from whom they were being removed was
Paul himself. He had called them into the grace of
Christ. They had loved him dearly, and now suddenly
under the spell of the law teachers, they considered him
almost an enemy. This is the evident meaning of "I
marvel that you are so soon removed from him." The
"him" was Paul himself. It does not refer to Christ, for
if really saved, they could not be "removed" from Him,
or separated. That, however, was the teaching of these
false prophets, that one could be joined to Christ, and
then be lost again. But that was the very error Paul was
seeking to correct in this epistle.

Paul is grieving over their loss of love for him by
being influenced by these proselyters, and bemoans the
fact they were so fickle. They had loved Paul so much
that they would have plucked out their own eyes, and
given them to him (Gal. 4:15). They had received him
as an angel of God (Gal. 4:14), and Paul asks in Galatians
4:15,

> Where is then the blessedness ye spake of? for I bear you
> record, that, if it had been possible, ye would have plucked
> out your own eyes, and have given them to me.
>
> Am I therefore become your enemy, because I tell you
> the truth?
>
> They (these proselyting legalists) zealously affect you, but
> not well; yea, they would exclude you, that ye might affect
> them (Gal. 4:15-17).

Where is your former love for me, who led you to
Christ by His grace? What made me your enemy now?
Is this the fruit of the false teaching you have now ac-
cepted concerning the law in your life? Paul says, "Don't

be carried away by their apparent zeal, if it does not promote love." He says, "They zealously affect you (you are impressed by their zeal)," but it is not good zeal, for they would separate friends, cause division, promote bigotry and intolerance. The verses may thus be translated: "These men (the Judaizing teachers) are zealously trying to dazzle you—paying court to you, making much of you, but their purpose is not honorable or worthy, or for any good. What they want to do is to isolate you (from us who oppose them) so that they may win you over to their side and get you to court their favor."

ANOTHER GOSPEL

Paul calls the teaching of these legalists ANOTHER GOSPEL. Their pious phrases sounded like the Gospel but it was not Paul's Gospel. Paul says ye are being removed from me who led you to Christ,

> . . . unto another gospel:
>   Which is not another; but there be some that trouble you, and would pervert the gospel of Christ (Gal. 1:6, 7).

The message these Judaizing teachers brought sounded very appealing and sound. There was so much truth mixed with error that the believers did not recognize the error. Their legalism was concealed with such a deceptive sugar-coating of Gospel phrases that the unsuspecting Galatians did not recognize the heresy. Just because men quote Scripture and talk about Jesus and grace and justification and faith does not mean anything, unless we also know what else they believe.

THE GREAT DECEPTION

These legalists who denied the message of Paul were clever deceivers. Paul refers to them as mesmerizers, enchanters, and bewitchers (Gal. 3:1). Paul pleads, therefore, that they be not deceived by their pious pratings and says, while it sounds like another Gospel, it is not the Gospel at all. You cannot mix law and grace, and faith and works. He says it—

> . . . is not another; but there be some that trouble you, and would pervert the gospel of Christ (Gal. 1:7).

I would have you notice one word in particular in verse 7. It is the word "pervert." It is "metastrepho" in the original and my Bible lexicon translates it as "to twist or distort." It is not a denial of the Gospel, but a twisting of the message. This twisting or distortion is accomplished by ADDING something to the grace of God. In the case of these false teachers, it was the preaching of grace—plus something. They preached the Gospel of grace, and something else. They taught that we are saved by grace—and then kept by works. This is called by Paul "another gospel, which is not another," but a perversion or distortion of the message of salvation.

Paul was so positive in this that he pens two of the most significant verses in all of his epistles. He says:

> But though we, or an angel from heaven, preach any other gospel unto you than that which we have preached unto you, let him be ACCURSED (Gal. 1:8).

This is strong language indeed. To be accursed is to be lost. Paul says to these Galatian Christians, the teachers who are attacking my Gospel of grace, who tell you that you are under the law for your salvation, who say that your salvation by grace depends upon your works after you are saved, that you can be saved by grace but only kept by works—these teachers, says Paul, are perverters of the Gospel and are still under the curse of the law. The law cannot save—it can only curse the sinner, and to place yourself under it is to place yourself under its curse. Paul is so sure of his ground that he repeats his startling condemnation in verse 9:

> As we said before, so say I now again, If any man preach any other gospel unto you than that ye have received (from me), let him be accursed (Gal. 1:9).

And what was the Gospel Paul preached? It was the message of grace. The test of the Gospel is GRACE. If you want to know if the message you hear is the Gospel, ask only one question, "Is it the message of grace—only grace—with nothing added?" Yes, the test of the Gospel is grace. If the message excludes grace, or mingles law with grace as the means of either justification or sanctification, it is another gospel. Paul sums it all up in Galatians 2:21,

> I do not frustrate the grace of God: for if righteousness come by the law, then Christ is dead in vain (Gal. 2:21).

What a terrible thing to say that our righteousness can be gained by lawkeeping. It accuses God of needlessly letting His Son be murdered without reason. The believer saved by the grace of God renounces all legal claim to the mercy of God, but accepts everything as a gift. If you work for a thing, then you earn it. If God saves you because of anything you DO, then God is indebted to you. Notice, in closing, Romans 4:4,

> Now to him that worketh is the reward not reckoned of grace, but of debt (Rom. 4:4).

If you can work for, or earn, your own salvation, or work to keep it, then God owes you salvation as wages, and you don't have to thank Him for it, because you earned it, and God owes it to you. Don't you see why God will not allow any man to work his way into Heaven? God does not give us a start for Heaven by grace, and then say, "Now keep going on your own power." That would give us something to crow about, saying, "Yes, God saved me, but I got here by hanging on."

Grace is the death of pride. It slays all self-exaltation. Nothing will humble a person like the grace of God, and when I see a proud Christian, I know he does not fully understand God's grace. There will be no strutting in Heaven. If the Lord would let you have anything to do with your salvation, you would be the biggest bore in Heaven. You would be a pest in boasting. Heaven would never hear the last of it. You would never get through telling about it. That is the reason, says Paul, why it is NOT OF WORKS—LEST ANY MAN SHOULD BOAST.

How precious the song by the late Dr. James M. Gray, former president of the Moody Bible Institute:

> Naught have I gotten but what I received;
>   Grace hath bestowed it since I have believed;
> Boasting excluded, pride I abase;
>   I'm only a sinner saved by grace!
> Suffer a sinner whose heart overflows,
>   Loving his Saviour to tell what he knows;
> Once more to tell it would I embrace—
>   I'm only a sinner saved by grace.

If it is not all of grace, then we are without a shred of hope or light for eternity.

Chapter Five

IN DEFENSE OF THE GOSPEL

> But I certify you, brethren, that the gospel which was preached of me is not after man.
>
> For I neither received it of man, neither was I taught it (by man), but by the revelation of Jesus Christ (Gal. 1:11, 12).

THE Apostle Paul was a most gracious, patient, sympathetic soul with a love for his enemies so great he could wish himself accursed from God to save them (Rom. 9:3). But while Paul was patient, loving, kind, tolerant and forbearing, he was no "softie" or "sissy." While he would arbitrate on non-essentials and would renounce his own liberties for the good of others, he was adamant in his stand for the truth. He would never compromise the truth of the Gospel. While gracious and tender in his dealings, there was one thing Paul would not tolerate. That one thing was tampering with the grace of God. On the matter of salvation by grace without the deeds of the law, he would give no quarter. He was stubbornly firm in his preaching that a man is saved and kept, justified and sanctified by grace—plus nothing. This tender apostle, therefore, could be the very essence of severity toward the false legalistic teachers who had upset the Galatian Christians by the false teaching that they were saved by grace, and then kept by works. Paul calls this a perverted gospel (Gal. 1:7) and pronounces the curse of God upon them and says:

> Though we, or an angel from heaven, preach any other gospel unto you than that which we have preached unto you, let him be accursed (Gal. 1:8).

NOT A MAN PLEASER

To the charge that Paul was mistaken in preaching grace, and deliverance from the law, Paul answers in Galatians 1:10,

> For do I now persuade men, or God? or do I seek to please men? for if I yet pleased men, I should not be the servant of Christ (Gal. 1:10).

Paul asks them, Do you think I am trying to please men or God? I could avoid all this persecution if I, like you, would bring a popular message of works and human merit and righteousness, but I would prove myself to be a false teacher. Paul had received his message direct from Heaven, and knew he was right. It was a new message, not fully set forth until now. The apostles in Jerusalem were still preaching the Kingdom message. They preached only to Jews, and not to the Gentiles. With the exception of Peter's use of the keys in the household of Cornelius in Acts 10, not a single one of the apostles in Jerusalem (including Peter) had preached to anyone but the Jews. When Paul therefore came with the message of grace to the Gentiles as well as the Jews, he met with violent opposition. The legalistic Judaizers followed him from place to place, seeking to turn the Gentile converts away from the message of Paul.

WHY THE OPPOSITION?

Paul was not accepted by these teachers as an apostle, because he had not been elected by the eleven. His teaching of grace was rejected because he did not get his training from the apostles in Jerusalem. His authority was questioned because he had not consulted the apostles in the church at Jerusalem. As a result Paul was constantly put on the defensive and called upon to prove his apostleship and his authority. There were three things which Paul had to defend:

1. His commission as an apostle.
2. His message of grace.
3. His ministry to the Gentiles.

His commission was questioned. They doubted his authority because he did not receive his credentials from the other apostles. Second, his message of grace, instead of the apostolic Kingdom message, was refuted and denied, and Galatians was written to defend his position. And thirdly, his ministry to the Gentiles was criticized because the apostles still did not seem to realize that the middle wall between Jew and Gentile was broken down. The Kingdom message had been rejected by the Nation, and the Kingdom was postponed, and therefore the gospel of the Kingdom was replaced during this dispensation by the message of grace to Jew and Gentile alike. For these three reasons Paul had to defend himself constantly against his critics. For his defense, Paul now demonstrates his position:

1. He calls the Galatians to witness to his sincerity. He says, You know me, that I am not a man pleaser, but seek to please God. My sojourn among you proves my authority (Gal. 1:10).

2. He boldly asserts that his authority is from God, and not from man (Gal. 1:11, 12).

3. He calls upon his past reputation as a legalistic Judaizer, and his miraculous conversion (Gal. 1:13).

4. He began his preaching of grace long before he had seen any of the apostles at Jerusalem, and this accounted

for the difference in the apostolic message of the Kingdom, and Paul's message of grace (Gal. 1:14, 15).

5. When Paul did confer with the apostles at Jerusalem, they could not give him any new truth to add to what Paul already knew (Gal. 1:16, 17).

6. The apostles had recognized Paul's distinctive ministry to the Gentiles, and agreed to it and endorsed his message (Gal. 2:7-10).

HIS DIVINE MESSAGE

Paul asserts his authority and the source of his revelation in verses 11 and 12:

> But I certify you, brethren, that the gospel which was preached of me is not after man.
>
> For I neither received it of man, neither was I taught it (by man), but by the revelation of Jesus Christ (Gal. 1:11, 12).

The Gospel Paul preached was a new revelation from Heaven. He presumably received it during his three years of schooling in Arabia after his conversion. Here Paul was caught up into Paradise and received revelations from God, much of which he was not even permitted to utter. These truths could not be found in the Old Testament Scriptures, for then it would not have been a revelation. Neither did Paul receive his message of grace from the apostles, for they themselves did not know it fully. It was a special revelation, a new thing, not known before. Of this Paul says in Ephesians 3:3,

> How that by revelation he (God) made known unto me the mystery; . . .
>
> Which in other ages was not made known unto the sons of men, as it is now revealed unto his holy apostles and prophets by the Spirit (Eph. 3:3, 5).

And what was the new revelation of the mystery? Here it is in Ephesians 3:6,

That the Gentiles should be fellowheirs, and of the same body, and partakers of his promise in Christ by the gospel.

This was the new revelation, and Paul asserts that this was committed to him specifically, and says:

. . . that I should preach among the GENTILES the unsearchable riches of Christ (Eph. 3:8).

This was something brand new. Up until now the message of God had been to one nation, Israel. The only way a Gentile could be saved was by becoming a Jew. He must become a proselyte, submit to the rite of circumcision and keep the Law of Moses. And now Paul comes with this message of free grace. Salvation is now extended to all. The Gentiles can be saved by grace without circumcision, without the law, without becoming Jews. No wonder it caused a stir of opposition. This was revolutionary truth, indeed, and had to be settled. This was the question before the first council in Jerusalem in Acts 15. Paul had preached the message of grace in Antioch and there was great joy among the believers UNTIL certain teachers (like the ones who came to disturb the Galatians) came up to corrupt the Gospel of grace. We read in Acts 15:1,

And certain men which came down from Judaea (to Antioch) taught the brethren, and said, Except ye be circumcised after the manner of Moses, ye cannot be saved.

When therefore Paul and Barnabas had no small dissension and disputation with them, they determined that Paul and Barnabas, and certain other of them, should go up to Jerusalem unto the apostles and elders about this question (Acts 15: 1, 2).

The happy assembly in Antioch had been thrown into turmoil by these proselyters of the law. There was NO SMALL dissension. It was a wild meeting and they proposed to consult the apostles. When they arrived in

Jerusalem the meeting was called, and what a time they had. Paul was put on the "pan" and accused of preaching a false gospel.

> But there rose up certain of the sect of the Pharisees which believed, saying, That it was needful to circumcise them (the Gentile believers), and to command them to keep the law of Moses (Acts 15:5).

That was the charge and immediately the fight began, and we read:

> And when there had been much disputing, Peter rose up (Acts 15:7).

He gives his testimony of what he had seen and pleads that they abandon their efforts to put the Gentiles under the law which they themselves could not keep. He concludes with the impassioned plea:

> Now therefore why tempt ye God, to put a yoke upon the neck of the disciples, which neither our fathers nor we were able to bear?
> But we believe that through the GRACE of the Lord Jesus Christ we shall be saved, even as they (Acts 15:10, 11).

After this, Paul recounts his experience. Then James, the chairman of the meeting, gives his opinion and says:

> Wherefore my sentence is, that we trouble not them, which from among the Gentiles are turned unto God (Acts 15:19).

It was finally decided that Paul was correct in preaching grace without the law, and that a letter be sent to the troubled believers at Antioch. The letter was brief, but explicit:

> . . . greeting unto the brethren which are of the Gentiles in Antioch and Syria and Cilicia:
> Forasmuch as we have heard, that certain which went out from us have troubled you with words, subverting your

souls, saying, Ye must be circumcised, and keep the law:
TO WHOM WE GAVE NO SUCH COMMANDMENT
(Acts 15:23, 24).

The verdict was—the Gentiles are not under the law.
Salvation is by the grace of God, wholly apart from works.
The matter was settled over nineteen hundred years ago
in Jerusalem and yet the disturbers of the peace who
followed Paul around to trouble his converts are still as
busy as ever, seeking to unsettle God's people with their
corrupted, perverted gospel of legalism. If they only
knew that they are not only corrupting the grace of God,
but placing themselves under the curse of God, they would
cast themselves upon the mercy of God, and escape the
curse of the law.

If salvation be by works of the law, then all are lost,
for the law demands continued, unbroken, perfect and
complete obedience to every precept of the law of God.
In closing we call attention to a most conclusive passage,
(Gal. 3:10-12):

> For as many as are of the works of the law are under the
> curse: for it is written, Cursed is EVERY ONE THAT
> CONTINUETH NOT IN ALL THINGS which are writ-
> ten in the book of the law to do them.
> But that no man is justified by the law in the sight of
> God, it is evident: for, The just shall live by faith.
> And the law is not of faith: but, The man that doeth
> them shall live in them.

To be saved by the law demands perfect, complete,
uninterrupted obedience. If this were possible for a
sinner, faith would be made void and the sacrifice of
Christ a needless, colossal blunder.

> If righteousness come by the law, then Christ is dead
> in vain (Gal. 2:21b).

Chapter Six

FREE FROM THE LAW

THE Apostle Paul claimed that he was caught up into Paradise and received his commission as the Apostle to the Gentiles directly from God. This claim of Paul was denied by the false teachers of the law, and Paul was constantly called upon to defend his authority. And even as his commission came direct from God, so Paul's message also was a new and direct revelation from God, not made known before to the children of men. It was the new message of the grace of God which Jesus had promised when He said:

> I have yet many things to say unto you, but ye cannot bear them now.
> Howbeit when he, the Spirit of truth, is come, he will guide you into all truth (John 16:12, 13).

This promise was fulfilled after Pentecost, and the revelation is recorded in the epistles of Paul, Peter, James, John and Jude. But it was especially through Paul that the new revelation of the grace of God was given. This Paul asserts repeatedly. He says:

> ... I neither received it of man, neither was I taught it, but by the revelation of Jesus Christ (Gal. 1:12).

God revealed to Paul that he was to preach the Gospel to the Gentiles and it was to be the message of grace. Listen to his testimony:

> But when it pleased God, who separated me from my mother's womb, and called me by his grace,

To reveal his Son in me, that I might preach him among the heathen (Gentiles); immediately I conferred not with flesh and blood:

Neither went I up to Jersualem to them which were apostles before me; but I went into Arabia, and returned again unto Damascus.

Then after three years (in Arabia) I went up to Jerusalem to see Peter, and abode with him fifteen days.

But other of the apostles saw I none, save James the Lord's brother (Gal. 1:15-19).

DIVINE REVELATION

Paul, in these verses, goes to great pains to show that his message was not from man. He did not receive it from the apostles, but directly from Heaven. After his conversion, instead of going for instruction to Jerusalem and the apostles, he went into Arabia, for three years of fundamental training. Here he received the revelation of the grace of God to the Gentiles. It was not the message of the apostles to Israel, but a new revelation of the mystery of the Body of Christ as composed of both Jew and Gentile. At the close of Paul's three years in Arabia he returned to Damascus. It was only after these three years in Arabia that Paul met Peter and James. He was with them only two weeks, but they could not add anything to what Paul had received.

It was this new revelation of Paul which was called in question and which he was constantly called upon to defend. Listen to his emphatic assertion in Galatians 1:20,

Now the things which I write unto you, behold, before God, I lie not (Gal. 1:20).

Paul affirms his stand with an oath, and calls God to witness the divine authority of his words. But while the Jews at Jerusalem opposed and rejected Paul, the Gentile believers rejoiced. After leaving Peter and James, Paul went into the regions of Syria and Cilicia. He abandoned the city of Jerusalem and remained a stranger to the disciples in Jerusalem and Judaea. He says he was:

> . . . unknown by face unto the churches of Judaea which were in Christ:
>
> But they had heard only, That he which persecuted us in times past now preacheth the faith which once he destroyed.
>
> And they glorified God in me (Gal. 1:22-24).

THE GREAT COUNCIL

Chapter two of Galatians opens with an account of the first great church council recorded in the fifteenth of Acts. The occasion was the controversy over the matter of circumcision and the Law of Moses. These legalistic disturbers of the peace from Judaea had come to Antioch and opposed Paul's message of grace, asserting that the Gentiles "must be circumcised (become Jews), and keep the law" (Acts 15:24). So serious was the dissension that a committee (including Paul and Barnabas) were delegated to go to Jerusalem to seek advice from the apostles.

This was seventeen years after Paul's conversion and he gives added details in this chapter (Galatians 2) of this meeting. We have already seen the final decision of the council in Acts 15:23-31. It was an endorsement of Paul's message of grace—salvation for Jew and Gentile by grace—without the works of the law. Here is Paul's own account:

> Then fourteen years after I went up again to Jerusalem with Barnabas, and took Titus with me also.
>
> And I went up by revelation, and communicated unto them that gospel which I preach among the Gentiles, but privately to them which were of reputation, lest by any means I should run, or had run, in vain (Gal. 2:1, 2).

PRIVATE MEETING

When Paul arrived at Jerusalem he first called for a
meeting with the leaders of the church, to reach an
understanding, and to be able to present a united front
before his critics. To these leaders Paul told of his experience. As a test he took Titus with him, a Gentile,
to see whether they would insist on his being circumcised
according to the law. The purpose was, of course, to
silence the false teachers who had come to the meeting
to destroy Paul's message. Paul says, he made the circumcision of Titus a test because—

> . . . of false brethren unawares brought in, who came in
> privily to spy out our liberty which we have in Christ Jesus,
> that they might bring us into bondage (Gal. 2:4).

But Paul was ready for them, and refused to budge
one inch from his position of grace. He says (verse 5):

> To whom we gave place by subjection, NO, not for an
> hour; that the truth of the gospel might continue with you
> (Gal. 2:5).

THE GREAT DECISION

Having silenced his enemies, he now convinces the
apostles of his specific commission and an amicable agreement is reached.

> But of these who seemed to be somewhat (prominent
> leaders in the church), . . . in conference added nothing to
> me (Gal. 2:6).

This conference with the apostles did not change Paul's
position in the least, but rather confirmed his stand.
Remember that there was a question about Paul's message of grace, because it seemed to conflict with the apostles' message of the Kingdom. Peter's message at Pentecost had been, ". . .Repent, and be baptized every one of
you in the name of Jesus Christ for the remission of sins,

and ye shall receive the gift of the Holy Ghost" (Acts 2:38). But Paul never preached that message. The message at Pentecost was to the Jews and the Nation of Israel. There was not a Gentile present—only Jews and proselytes (Acts 2:10). Peter preached baptism for the remission of sins. But Paul's message was, "Believe on the Lord Jesus Christ, and thou shalt be saved" (Acts 16:31). And then baptism followed as a testimony of faith. In Peter's message baptism preceded the remission of sins; in Paul's message water baptism followed conversion.

THE PROBLEM

Now who was right, Peter or Paul? This question can only be answered if we distinguish between the dispensation of the Law which ended at Calvary, and the dispensation of the Grace of God which began after Pentecost. Peter was converted before the dispensation of the Law ended; Paul was saved after the dispensation of Grace began. He called the revelation he received the "dispensation of grace" (Eph. 3:2). Now many people throw up their hands in holy horror at the preaching of dispensational truth, but beloved, there is no other way to understand the Bible. How else can we harmonize the message of Peter and the message of Paul? We must distinguish God's dealings in the dispensations. Notice the contrast between the dispensations of law and grace. Under the law a stubborn, rebellious son was stoned (Deut. 21:18). Under grace the prodigal son is welcomed and forgiven by the father (Luke 15:20). Under the law a man who gathered sticks on the sabbath day to cook a bit of food was stoned to death (Num. 15:35). Under grace we are in the perfect liberty of the Gospel and serve the Lord not by threat of death, but because of the promise of life. If everyone who turned on the gas yesterday (the Saturday sabbath) to warm their food, or turned on the lights in the house, were stoned to death, the undertakers would be swamped. Yet that is what the Law demanded. Under the law a woman caught in the act of adultery was to be put to death (Lev. 20:10). Under grace, forgiveness is granted and the woman admonished with the words of forgiveness from Jesus' lips, "Neither do I condemn thee: go, and sin no more" (John 8:11). How can we reconcile these two wholly different treatments of the same sins? Does God have a double standard? Or has God changed His mind? The only answer can be found in recognizing God's dispensational dealing under the Age of Law and the Age of Grace. Dispensational teaching—rightly dividing the Word—is the only way to understand the Bible. Failure to rightly divide the dispensations closes the door to rightly understand the grace of God.

PETER AND PAUL

This too is the answer to the difference in the ministry of Peter and Paul. Peter had received the Kingdom message from Christ (Matt. 10). It was limited to Israel, and offered the Kingdom, upon condition of national repentance. But Israel rejected the offer and refused the Messiah, and so the Kingdom offer is temporarily withdrawn, the Kingdom is postponed, and the ministry of Peter and the apostles comes to an end, and God now reveals the new message of grace for the Church Age, the Body of Christ. He chooses Paul to be the instrument for this new message to the Gentiles. The apostles now fade out of the picture and Paul takes over and dominates the rest of the Book of Acts from chapters 16 to 24.

At the church council in Jerusalem (Acts 15) where this dispensational question was discussed, an agreement was reached to the satisfaction of all. We can do no better than read it as Paul has recorded it for us. After Paul had successfully beaten off his accusers, to whom he yielded not an inch, we read:

> . . . when they (the apostles) saw that the gospel of the uncircumcision (grace, to the Gentiles) was committed unto me, as the gospel of the circumcision (the Kingdom message to Israel) was (committed) unto Peter;
>
> (For he that wrought effectually in Peter to the apostleship of the circumcision (Israel), the same was mighty in me toward the Gentiles:)
>
> And when James, Cephas (Peter), and John, who seemed to be pillars, perceived the grace that was given unto me, they gave to me and Barnabas the right hands of fellowship; that we should go unto the heathen (Gentiles), and they unto the circumcision (Gal. 2:7-9).

Now that should have settled the matter. Paul was to go to the Gentiles, Peter and the apostles to Israel. But the dispensation of the Law had ended, Israel was set aside, until the Church Age should be completed. Hence the Kingdom message to Israel is withdrawn, until God again begins to deal with the nation, after this Church Age. We are now in the dispensation of Grace— the dispensation of Law has ended. And so Peter and the apostles with their ministry to Israel disappear from view. The last we hear of them is in Acts 15, and we hear no more about them. Only after the Church is gone will the Kingdom message be resumed, Israel shall be saved, and the glorious Messianic Kingdom be ushered in, and the apostles' ministry begin once again (Matt. 19:28).

In closing, let us gather up the message. The message for this age is, "Believe on the Lord Jesus Christ, and thou shalt be saved and thy house." To place oneself under the law is to return to the curse and be lost. The sinner is saved by grace WITHOUT THE DEEDS OF THE LAW, and the believer is kept by the grace of God WITHOUT THE DEEDS OF THE LAW. In our next message we shall see Paul's testimony in Galatians 2:19,

> For I through the law am dead to the law, that I might live unto God (Gal. 2:19).

> For Christ is the end of the law . . . to every one that believeth (Rom. 10:4).

Are you trying to merit salvation and earn Heaven by your own efforts and law-works? You'll never make it! Come as a poor, paupered, bankrupt beggar and say:

> Rock of Ages, cleft for me,
>   Let me hide myself in Thee;
> Let the water and the blood,
>   From Thy riven side which flowed,
> Be of sin the double cure,
>   Save me from its guilt and power.

> Not the labors of my hands
>   Can fulfill Thy law's demands;
> Could my zeal no respite know,
>   Could my tears forever flow,
> All for sin could not atone;
>   Thou must save, and Thou alone.

Chapter Seven

DEAD TO THE LAW

THE Apostle Paul was not an ordained minister in the ecclesiastically accepted sense. He did not receive his theological training in a denominational seminary. He had no degrees, earned, honorary, or otherwise. He was not ordained by an official council or synod or conference. He could produce no diploma from some great theological institution. He had not been licensed to preach by a committee of elders, bishops, or presbyters. He belonged to no ministerial association. There is no record that he was ever called "Reverend" or "Doctor" or "Dominie" or "Parson." He never signed his name, Rev. Doctor Paul, D.D. Because of these facts Paul was rejected by the religious legalists of his day. He was not a product of their seminary, had not been licensed or ordained by their church group, he was not a member of their association, and so they would exclude him. Paul had received his commission and his message of grace direct from Heaven. This was not the message which Peter and the apostles had been commissioned to preach exclusively to Israel. That message was "Repent ye, for the kingdom of heaven is at hand" (Matt. 10:7). It was the Kingdom message to Israel only. Paul's message to the Gentiles, however, was, "Believe on the Lord Jesus Christ, and thou shalt be saved, and thy house" (Acts 16:31). Because of this, a dispute arose in Antioch over this apparent conflict of messages, and a committee was sent to the apostles in Jerusalem to settle the matter.

THE VERDICT

The conclusion reached after much debating was that God had called Peter to minister to the Nation of Israel, but Paul was commissioned as the "apostle to the Gentiles" (Rom. 11:13). It was decided that Paul should go to the heathen, and they (the apostles) "unto the circumcision" (Gal. 2:9). Peter and the apostles gave the right hand of fellowship and acknowledged the authority of the Gospel of grace, that there was no difference between Jew and Gentile, but in this dispensation all must be saved alike, BY GRACE THROUGH FAITH, without the deeds of the Law.

BUT! BUT!

It seemed the matter was settled, and Peter, rejoicing in his new-found liberty of grace, decided to go to Antioch and visit the Gentile Christians, and there demonstrated his agreement with Paul. But something happened in Antioch which so violently incensed the Apostle Paul against Peter that he openly rebukes him before all, and exclaims in the most daring, remarkable declaration, his own personal relationship to the Law, and says:

For I through the law am dead to the law (Gal. 2:19).

What a tremendous statement! Paul does not say the law is dead. Far from it, but he says, "I am dead to the law." He is speaking of God's holy, inviolable law, including the Commandments written upon the tables of stone, and says, as far as that law is concerned, I am dead. In the eyes of the law, I don't even exist any more. The law does not even recognize my existence. So little power, so little application has that law to me. Let me repeat,

Paul does not say, "the law is dead." It is very, very much alive. It still curses, it still condemns the sinner, it still is the ministration of death. It still demands the death of the transgressor. But says Paul: as far as I am concerned the law cannot touch me any more. I am beyond its reach forever, for "I through the law am dead to the law."

Now, what is true of Paul is true of every believer. In Romans 7:4 we read:

> Wherefore, my brethren, ye also are become dead to the law by the body of Christ.

And again in Romans 6:14 we read:

> . . . for ye are not under the law, but under grace.

DEAD TO THE LAW

Yes, says Paul, I am dead to the law, but alive unto God. These remarkable words of Paul were spoken in response to a certain inconsistent conduct on the part of the Apostle Peter at Antioch. Paul had preached grace, grace; salvation wholly apart from the law; salvation by faith in the finished work of the Lord Jesus Christ. He had taught that the Gentile believers were not under the law, but were saved by grace, sanctified by grace, and kept by grace. Peter also when he came up to Antioch from Jerusalem, endorsed this stand of Paul and entered into the full fellowship of these Gentile believers on the basis of grace alone.

Then some legalistic, proselyting law preachers came up from Jerusalem in order to spy out Paul's liberty, and Peter, fearing their disfavor, immediately became scared and withdrew himself from these Gentiles, and put himself back under the law. This so incensed Paul that he openly rebuked Peter, and he really "dressed him down" for his inconsistency. Peter's error was a double standard of conduct for Jew and Gentile. With the Jews he placed himself under law; with the Gentiles he took his place under grace.

This brought forth Paul's severe rebuke. But let Paul tell it himself, in Galatians 2:12-16,

> For before that certain came from James, he (Peter) did eat with the Gentiles; but when they were come, he withdrew and separated himself, fearing them which were of the circumcision.
>
> And the other Jews dissembled likewise with him; insomuch that Barnabas also was carried away with their dissimulation.
>
> But when I saw that they walked not uprightly according to the truth of the gospel, I said unto Peter before them all, If thou, being a Jew, livest after the manner of Gentiles, and not as do the Jews, why compellest thou the Gentiles to live as do the Jews?
>
> We who are Jews by nature, and not sinners of the Gentiles,
>
> Knowing that a man is not justified by the works of the law, but by the faith of Jesus Christ, even we have believed in Jesus Christ, that we might be justified by the faith of Christ, and not by the works of the law: for by the works of the law shall no flesh be justified (Gal. 2:12-16).

It is after this that Paul gives his testimony climaxing in Galatians 2:19, and says: As for me personally, Peter—as for my relationship to the law, "I through the law am dead to the law, that I might live unto God."

AN ILLUSTRATION

What did Paul mean by the expression, "I am dead to the law"? An illustration or two, I am sure, will make it perfectly clear. Suppose a man has committed a terrible crime, let us say the crime of murder. He has deserved the penalty of the law which is life imprisonment or death. He therefore is arrested and brought into court before the judge, and indicted for murder. The witnesses are called, one by one, and all testify with one accord to the man's guilt. There seems to be no defense for him at all. He is guilty and according to the law should be put to death. But, before sentence is pronounced upon the man, or the trial is over, something suddenly happens to him. While he is on the stand during the trial, the man suddenly grasps his throat, his face becomes blue, his eyes bulge out, he stiffens in every muscle, and then suddenly slumps down in his chair and passes out. The physician is called, and pronounces the criminal officially, legally dead.

Now what does the judge do? Does he continue the trial? Does he continue to hear the rest of the testimonies? Of course not. The law cannot try a dead man. It applies only to living men. The man is dead. He is beyond the reach of the law, and so the judge raps his gavel, and solemnly announces the case dismissed and the court adjourned. The man is dead, dead in the eyes of the law. The law cannot try a dead man.

PAUL DIED TOO

Now that is the statement Paul makes: "I am dead to the law." But in the case of our illustration the man cheated the law. He robbed the law of its right to put him to death. He died before the law could exact its penalty. The man cheated the law by dying before the law could do to him what it had a perfect right to do; namely, to put him to death.

DEAD THROUGH THE LAW

In the case of Paul it was quite different. Paul was, indeed, dead to the law, but the law itself had put him to death. Notice, therefore, in our text, Galatians 2:19, that Paul added three words: THROUGH THE LAW. He not only said, "I am dead TO the law," but he says, "I THROUGH THE LAW am dead to the law." Don't miss those three words, THROUGH THE LAW. Yes, Paul is indeed dead to the law, but it was the law itself which executed him and put him to death.

ANOTHER ILLUSTRATION

Let me illustrate again. Here again is our criminal, guilty of a capital crime. He is indicted, brought to trial and the witnesses are called and all with one accord testify to the man's guilt. The defense sums up its case; and the prosecutor sums up his, and demands the death of the criminal. He is found guilty by the court, guilty of first degree murder, and on the day of sentence the judge pronounces solemn judgment and says to the guilty man, "The law decrees that on next Thursday you shall be hung by the neck until you are dead." And so Thursday comes, the man is led from his cell, walks up the thirteen steps, the black hood is placed over his head, and the noose is placed about his neck. At the signaled moment the trap door is sprung, the man hurtles down, till he reaches the end of the rope. His neck snaps, his face grows livid and in a few moments the body hangs limp upon the gallows. The physician enters and pronounces him legally and officially dead. It is so recorded in the law books. The law has been fully satisfied now. It can do no more, and it will ask no more. The case is closed.

DEAD BOTH TO AND THROUGH THE LAW

You see, this man now is not only dead TO the law, but he is dead THROUGH the law. The law has put

him to death. But now listen, for a strange thing happens.
Three days later you meet this same man, who died
through the law, walking alive on the streets of your
city. You cannot believe your eyes at first, so you look
again; but, yes, it is the same identical man. You are
sure. And so you rush to the police and then to the judge,
and you shout, "Get out the police force. Pick up that
murderer. He is running loose upon the streets of our
city." But the judge is quite unimpressed. He says, "Wait
a minute till I look up the record," and he opens the
books and finds the man is dead, legally dead to the law.
The fact that the man arose again after three days is of
no concern to the law. The law did not anticipate a resurrection. It made no provision beyond death. It is interested only in the death of the criminal, and there its
power and interest entirely stops. And so the judge says,
"Sorry, the man is legally dead. He has paid his debt to
society. I find nothing in the law which can judge a dead
man, nor do I find anything in the law that can punish
a man twice for the same crime." The law does not cover
or mention a resurrection. It stops at the grave.

That is what Paul says, and means in the testimony of
Galatians 2:19,

> For I through the law am dead to the law, that I might live
> unto God.

How could Paul say that? If you will read the next
verse, Galatians 2:20, you will have the answer as Paul
gives it himself. Study this verse, memorize it before
reading the next chapter. It tells us how Paul actually
became dead to the law and alive unto God. Here is
that wonderful verse which we quote so very, very often,
and yet take it out of its connection with the 19th verse.
Here is Galatians 2:20,

I am crucified with Christ: nevertheless I live; yet not I, but Christ liveth in me: and the life which I now live in the flesh I live by the faith of the Son of God, who loved me, and gave himself for me.

I do not frustrate the grace of God: for if righteousness come by the law, then Christ is dead in vain (Gal. 2:20, 21).

Marvelous is the explanation which Paul gives. He says, I died in the person of the Lord Jesus Christ, through faith I was identified with Him, so that God imputes to me everything that happened to the Saviour in whom I have put my trust; and since He met all the demands of the law, paid the penalty and died under its curse, I (because I was represented in Christ through grace) suffered the same penalty and God today considers me as though I actually, personally, hung on the Cross myself, and met the full penalty of the law, which is eternal death. That is Paul's testimony, and every believer who is in Christ can truly say, I too am crucified with Christ, nevertheless I live.

> Free from the law, O happy condition!
> Jesus has died, and there is remission.
> Cursed by the law, Ruined by the fall.
> Christ has redeemed us, Once for all.
> Once for all, Oh, sinner, receive it.
> Once for all, Oh, doubter, believe it.
> Come to the Cross, the burden will fall.
> Christ has redeemed us, Once for all.

Chapter Eight

CRUCIFIED WITH CHRIST

> For I through the law am dead to the law, that I might live unto God (Gal. 2:19).

"IS the Christian under the law?" This was already a burning question in the days of Paul; and although the Bible is crystal-clear in the answer that was given under inspiration by the Holy Spirit, (that the believer is not under the law, but under grace), yet proud-hearted man will not accept God's grace, but would rather try to save himself by his own goodness and works.

And that is just exactly what Satan wants man to do. Satan, the enemy of our souls, wants us to be religious and morally good. He urges men to strive to improve themselves, to try and obey the law, to keep on working and toiling, to be earnest and sincere and religious in all their efforts at keeping the commandments and the Sabbath days in an effort to make themselves worthy of God's favor instead of accepting His grace. But Paul says this is another gospel, and just a clever trick of the enemy of our souls to keep us from coming to the Christ of grace as poor, hopeless, helpless sinners. The law, says Paul, was given not to save, but to show the awfulness of sin, and our need of salvation.

To the question then, "Is the believer under the law?" Paul declares, "Absolutely NOT!" The believer is not under the law, but grace (Rom. 6:14). He is loosed

from the law (Rom. 7:2). He is delivered from the law
(Rom. 7:6). Christ is the end of the law to everyone that
believeth (Rom. 10:4). The Christian is free from the
law (Rom. 8:2), and in our Scripture, Galatians 2:19,
Paul declares, "I am dead to the law."

WHERE DID YOU DIE?

"But Paul, listen to me; when and where did you die,
and how were you executed?" The answer is in Galatians
2:19, 20. We must read the two verses together:

> . . . I through the law am dead to the law, that I might
> live unto God (Gal. 2:19).

And then Paul immediately explains how, where, and
when he died, and says:

> I am (have been) crucified with Christ: nevertheless I
> live (Gal. 2:20).

I died by crucifixion on a Cross upon a hill outside of
Jerusalem. Now in order to understand Paul's words,
"I am crucified with Christ," we need to remind you of
what God saw in Christ as His Son hung upon that Cross.

THE BODY OF CHRIST

As Jesus hung on the Cross, men saw only a man,
a human body with nails through His hands and His
feet. But as God looked down upon His Son, He saw far
more than a physical body; He also saw a spiritual Body,
a mystical Body, which is the Body of Christ. This
spiritual, mystical Body is the Church of the living God
with every member represented in that Body.

God looks upon the Church as a Body, Christ as the
Head, and we as the members. In I Corinthians 12:13
we read:

> For by one Spirit are we all baptized into one body,
> whether we be Jews or Gentiles.

And again, in Ephesians 5:30 we read:

> For we are members of his body, of his flesh, and of his bones.

And again, in Colossians 1:18 we read:

> And he is the head of the body, the church: who is the beginning, the firstborn from the dead; that in all things he might have the preeminence.

Christ then is the Head and we are the members of His Body. And so as God looked down upon the Lord Jesus Christ on the Cross, He saw not only the Head but the entire Body with all of its members. He saw the Church which is His Body; and that which happened to that Body, therefore, on the Cross, God reckoned as having happened to every member in that Body. From eternity God saw that Body, the Church, and saw every member of that Body before Him. God is timeless. God has no past. God has no future. He lives in the eternal present. Time is a creature-concept, but God knows no time, but all things are with Him as though they already existed. God is also omniscient. He knows all things beforehand. From eternity the Body of Christ was already complete in the mind of God, and He saw every member, every believer, every saved person in that Body, before He even created the world. In the mind of God our salvation was already completed before the worlds were made. And with God, Jesus was already "The Lamb slain from (before) the foundation of the world" (Rev. 13:8). And in the mind of God we were already members of the Body of Christ before creation. He foresaw, He foreknew each one, according to Ephesians 1, verse 3, where we read:

> Blessed be the God and Father of our Lord Jesus Christ, who hath blessed us with all spiritual blessings in heavenly places in Christ:

According as he hath chosen us in him before the foundation of the world, that we should be holy and without blame before him in love:

Having predestinated us unto the adoption of children by Jesus Christ to himself, according to the good pleasure of his will (Eph. 1:3-5).

IN CHRIST

As God therefore looked down upon Jesus on the Cross, He saw the Body of Christ, He saw every member of that Body. He saw Paul, He saw me, He saw you if you are a believer, and He reckoned that what happened to that Body happened to all the members of that Body, for we are members of His Body.

This then is the meaning of the words of Paul, "For I through the law am dead to the law," and it was through death by crucifixion. Through grace Paul was IN CHRIST as He hung on the Cross, and what happened to Jesus happened to him, for he was IN Christ. God accepted the death of Christ in full payment of the law's penalty for every member in that Body. If Paul personally, in his own physical body, had died the death on the Cross, it could have been no more real than his death TO the law, and THROUGH the law by the Body of Christ. That is why Paul says in Romans 7, verse 4:

Wherefore, my brethren, ye also are become dead to the law by the BODY of Christ.

The law could do no more. "I am dead to the law," says Paul. "I was crucified with Christ," but there is still more.

BURIED WITH CHRIST

After Jesus died on the Cross, two men, Joseph of Arimathaea and Nicodemus, went to Pilate and requested the body of the Lord for burial. Here is the record coning Joseph of Arimathaea:

He went to Pilate, and begged the body of Jesus. Then Pilate commanded the body to be delivered.

And when Joseph had taken the body, he wrapped it in a clean linen cloth,

And laid it in his own new tomb (Matt. 27:58-60).

Will you please notice, three times, no less than THREE times, the word BODY is used in these three verses. Now remember, "We are members of His Body, of his flesh and of his bones." When they therefore buried the Saviour, they buried both the Head and the Body. Only as we realize this mystical relationship of the believer to Christ can we understand Paul's words in Romans 6:3,

Know ye not, that so many of us as were baptized into Jesus Christ were baptized into his death?

Therefore we are buried with him by baptism into death: that like as Christ was raised up from the dead by the glory of the Father, even so we also should walk in newness of life (Rom. 6:3, 4).

Yes, we are crucified with Christ, but we are also buried with Him, in the baptism of His death.

RAISED WITH CHRIST

But that is not all. There is still more. We are also raised with Him, for Paul says:

For I through the law am dead to the law, that I might LIVE unto God (Gal. 2:19).

"I am crucified with Christ: nevertheless I live," says Paul in the next verse. Yes, when the Lord Jesus arose, the whole Body arose. Every member of that Body came forth out of the tomb. We have been raised with Christ. Listen again to Paul in Romans 6:8,

Now if we be dead with Christ, we believe that we shall also live with him:

> Knowing that Christ being raised from the dead dieth
> no more; death hath no more dominion over him.
> For in that he died, he died unto sin once: but in that
> he liveth, he liveth unto God.
> Likewise reckon ye also yourselves to be dead indeed
> unto sin, but alive unto God through Jesus Christ our
> Lord (Rom. 6:8-11).

This very fact, that we are raised with Christ, free from
the law of sin and death, not in any sense under the law
at all any more, then becomes our incentive, our motive,
for holy living. The claim God has upon us is this: that
we are under grace, and so Paul says in Colossians 3:1,

> If ye then be risen with Christ, seek those things which
> are above, where Christ sitteth on the right hand of God.
> Set your affection on things above, not on things on
> the earth.
> For ye are dead, and your life is hid with Christ in
> God (Col. 3:1-3).

ASCENDED AND SEATED WITH CHRIST

But there is still more. We are not only crucified with
Christ, buried with Christ, raised with Christ, but in Him
we are already seated in the heavenlies. Though we are
still here in OUR bodies on earth, in the Body of the
Lord Jesus we are already in Heaven. When forty days
after His resurrection, Jesus ascended into Heaven, the
Head and the Body ascended together. The Body of
Christ is in Heaven today, and therefore, we may reckon
ourselves as members of His Body as already seated in
the heavenlies.

That too is Paul's assertion in that tremendous and
remarkable statement in Ephesians 2, verses 4 to 6:

> But God, who is rich in mercy, for His great love where-
> with he loved us,
> Even when we were dead in sins, hath quickened us
> together with Christ, (by grace ye are saved;)

And hath raised us up together, and made us sit together in heavenly places in Christ Jesus (Eph. 2:4-6).

What a remarkable statement, and what a glorious truth! What a wonderful position is ours! How sad, how tragic, that many, many professing Christians not understanding the grace of God, but being misled by the teaching that they are still under the law of commandments, worry, struggle, work and toil to keep saved, when if they only knew the truth of grace they would realize that they are already in Heaven in Christ, seated in the heavenlies.

Our Head Is in Heaven

Spurgeon once said, "As long as your head is above water you cannot drown the feet." Our Head truly is in Heaven now, having ascended, and we are members of His Body, of His flesh and of His bones.

Shall We Sin?

Now I hear someone say, "that is a terrible, a dangerous doctrine which leads to irresponsible and loose living. If by grace we are saved and forever secure in Christ, then it follows that we can live as we please, and it makes no difference."

Those of us who preach the free grace of God and salvation by faith, and freedom from the law and its curse, are constantly accused of this, that the teaching of grace makes for looseness of living, and gives us license to sin. However, we are not the first ones to be so accused, for Paul already had to face that same false charge because he too preached grace just as we seek to do. The legalists and the zealots for the law of Paul's day accused him also of teaching that freedom from the law gave him the right to live in sin and immorality. Those who reason thus have never learned the meaning of Grace.

Because we are not under THE law does not make us lawless, but we are placed under a new law—the law of life. And so Paul adds, "I am dead to the law, but ALIVE unto God." Delivered from the law of death, and placed under the law of life and love! This we take up in our next message. The proof of our deliverance from the law is our LIVING for God. The people who say, "Since we are not under the law, we can live as we want to," know nothing of the grace of God. Christ living in us, performs in us what the law was unable to accomplish. Let me close with Romans 8:3,

> For what the law could not do, in that it was weak through the flesh, God sending his own Son in the likeness of sinful flesh, and for sin, condemned sin in the flesh:
> That the righteousness of the law might be fulfilled IN US (Rom. 8:3, 4).

Chapter Nine

THE LAW OF LOVE

THE believer in Christ is not under the law, but under grace (Rom. 6:14). The believer is dead to the law (Gal. 2:19). The believer is free from the law (Rom. 7:3, 4). He is delivered from the law (Rom. 7:6). And in Romans 10:4 we read:

> For Christ is the end of the law for righteousness to every one that believeth (Rom. 10:4).

If there was any one single thing which Paul was dead set against, it was against being put back under the law from which he had been delivered by the grace of God. For many years Paul had lived under the law of Moses, and had done his very utmost extended best to keep that law in all sincerity, so that he could say, "as touching the law, blameless." And yet at the end of all those years of struggling to keep the law he found himself a poor lost sinner standing in the need of the mercy and the grace of God. Paul knew the utter futility of trying to please God by his own works, and therefore was ready to fight to the finish those who would bring him back under the bondage of the law.

The law cannot punish a man twice for the same crime, and since Christ paid the penalty for our sins and satisfied the whole law, His righteousness is now imputed to us and Christ is the "end of the law to every one that believeth."

Well, someone objects immediately, that's a dangerous doctrine. You say you are free from the law; it has no more claim upon you. Yes, that is the clear teaching of the Bible. Does this mean you can do as you please; you can be lawless and commit sin and it will make no difference at all? Not at all! Such language reveals total ignorance about the grace of God. We are free from the law of commandments, but not lawless, for we are now under another law, a better law, the law of love and devotion; yea, the royal law of liberty. Paul says in Romans:

> . . . ye also are become dead to the law by the body of Christ; that ye should be married to another, even to him who is raised from the dead (Rom. 7:4).

For this reason Paul says in Galatians 2:19, "For I through the law am dead to the law, that I might LIVE unto God."

Life takes the place of death. Love takes the place of the law. Where there is perfect love you need no law, for love goes way beyond the demands of the law. Allow me to give you a homely but pertinent illustration. Take a home where love reigns and each lives for the other. How much law do you find there?

Imagine for a moment that I am about to leave my home, and before I go, I put up a great big sign, several feet square, in the kitchen where it is very prominent. Then when I am ready to go away, I call my wife and say, "Now, Mrs. De Haan, listen to me, your boss. You see those rules up there. There are ten of them. They are your ten commandments by which you are to live in this home." And then follow the commandments:

Commandment No. 1—Thou shalt entertain no other husbands besides me.

Commandment No. 2—Thou shalt not run around gadding, or love anyone else more than me.

Commandment No. 3—Thou shalt not speak lightly or disparagingly about me, your husband, or take my name in vain.

Commandment No. 4—Thou shalt properly clothe and feed my children, and not allow them to starve.

Commandment No. 5—Thou shalt keep the house clean, and not sweep the dust under the rug.

And so on, and so on, I could go through the whole ten commandments, and I warn her and say, "Failure to observe these rules will result in your being severely punished by me, your husband. I may even divorce you."

Now do you think that I need that kind of a sign for my wife in my home? Do I have to lay down one single law? I should say not! And why not? Simply because she loves me. She is under the law of love. She loves her home, she loves her children, she delights in doing things for us, because she loves us. And so I have no laws tacked up in our kitchen, but when I get ready to leave, we kneel together in prayer, I give her a good hug and a real big kiss, and I am off, with never a care or a worry about my home, or the conduct of Mrs. De Haan.

She is not under law. If she were a servant, then we would need rules, regulations and laws. We would have to set working hours, wages, time off, and a hundred different rules, because a servant works for wages, but a wife works through love. We have no time clocks to punch in our home, no laws or rules for wages, or hours.

This, beloved, is the service that God desires of us. I do pity the poor, poor Christian who serves God through fear, through the threatenings of the law and the Ten Commandments, and the fear of chastening. That is a mean, low, base, unworthy motive for service. I pity the person who serves the Lord and works and strives for holiness, because he is afraid if he doesn't, he'll lose his salvation in the end. That is a mean, low, unworthy motive for service to God.

The service God expects is the service of love and devotion, gratitude for having saved us by His grace, and for having delivered us from the curse of the law.

THE LAW OUR GUIDE?

Now I hear someone say, "Yes, that is all right. I agree that we are justified by faith through grace and not works, but while we are not under the law, do we not need it as our pattern and guide to show us how to live AFTER WE ARE SAVED?" That is a legitimate question, but the answer is very clear in Scripture. When the poor sinner believes on Jesus Christ, he is born again; that is, BORN FROM ABOVE. The Holy Spirit moves in and takes possession of that life and forevermore dwells within that believer. We become temples of the Holy Ghost, and that perfect Spirit of God then becomes our guide, through the Word, for all future conduct and behavior. You have within you a PERSON who will tell you the right and the wrong. When temptation comes the believer does not have to run to the 20th chapter of Exodus and read the law to know what is right. He has within him One who will guide him into all truth. One Scripture will settle this point, I am sure. Here it is:

> For the grace of God that bringeth salvation hath appeared to all men,

> Teaching us that, denying ungodliness and worldly lusts,
> we should live soberly, righteously, and godly, in this present
> world (Titus 2:11, 12).

How would it sound if we read that verse this way: "For
the law of Moses that bringeth salvation hath appeared
to all men, teaching us that denying ungodliness—" No.
NO, NO! The grace of God teaches us to live for Him.
The Christian's guide through the Holy Spirit is:
"Whether therefore ye eat, or drink, or whatsoever ye
do, do all to the glory of God" (I Cor. 10:31).

I hear another say, "But do we not need the law today
to show us how terrible sin is? You say that was its mission
for Israel. Do not we need it today?" Do we? Is the best
picture of sin found in the LAW? It was once, but since
Calvary all this is different. If I want to see what sin
REALLY IS, I go, not to Mt. Sinai, but to Mt. Calvary.
There upon a cruel Cross of wood hangs a Man—nay,
more than a Man—the Son of God, the Creator of the
worlds. In Him was no sin, and in His mouth no guile.
He had never done aught but good. He had perfectly
kept God's holy law. He had not harmed anyone. Yet
there He hangs nailed by human hands to the Cross, the
symbol of the curse. His back is raw and the body torn
where the scourger's whip has pulled away the flesh
until the ribs are made bare and He could say, "I tell
all my bones." His face is red from the striking of vulgar
court hands. On His head is a crown of thorns, while
slowly trickling from the hundred thorny wounds is His
sinless blood. It trickles past His sunken eyes and con-
geals upon His cheeks to mingle with the filthy spittle of
an indiscriminate mob who had beaten Him and spit
upon Him. His lips are thin and blue and pinched.
Through His hands and feet are cruel nails, which pull

and tug excruciatingly at His flesh, as the weight of His body tears the wounds deeper and deeper. His skin is burning in the sunlight, until God Himself can behold the agony no longer and lowers the shades of heaven, blows out the lights of the firmament and turns His back upon His Son as the awful piercing cry rings out, "MY GOD, MY GOD, WHY HAST THOU FORSAKEN ME?" That man is perfect Man, and perfect God. Yet He hangs on the Cross bleeding, suffering, dying . . . WHY? WHY? . . . Why must He hang there? Hear the answer . . . SIN. SIN! My SIN and your SIN. So awful is sin that when Jesus took our sin upon Himself even God could not save His own dear Son. Ah, friend, if I want to see what sin is, I need not go all the way back to Sinai. I stop at Calvary and there I see in all its lurid reality what SIN IS and WHAT SIN DOES.

> It was for crimes that I had done,
>   He groaned upon the tree.
> Amazing pity! grace unknown
>   And love beyond degree!
>
> See, from His head, His hands, His feet,
>   Sorrow and love flow mingled down;
> Did e'er such love and sorrow meet,
>   Or thorns compose so rich a crown?

If a human being could possibly keep the law of God perfectly, then why did Jesus have to suffer all this for us? This too is the argument of Paul in Galatians 3:21, 22.

> Is the law then against the promises (the gospel) of God? God forbid: for if there had been a law given which could have given life, verily righteousness should have been by the law.
> But the scripture hath concluded all under sin, that the

promise by faith of Jesus Christ might be given to them that BELIEVE (Gal. 3:21, 22).

If the law could have given life, says Paul, then Christ would never have needed to die. If a man can save himself, then why does he need a Saviour to die in his place? If a man can keep himself saved, then why does he need a High Priest to intercede daily for him at the right hand of God? No, indeed, says Paul, the law and the Gospel are not against each other, but they do have entirely different purposes. The law slays and kills the sinner, that he may turn from the law and his own works to the Christ who alone can give him life.

Nowhere is this better stated than in Galatians 2:21 where Paul says:

> I do not frustrate the grace of God: for if righteousness come by the law, then Christ is dead in vain (Gal. 2:21).

That is a tremendous statement—"then Christ is dead in vain." Then His death was all of no avail, if man can save or keep himself by the works of the law. To cling to the law, to turn again to the commandments, is to deny the sacrifice of Christ, and it brings us again under the curse of God.

By our admission that we cannot by ourselves keep God's holy law, we prove its perfection. To say that we can keep God's holy law is to drag that holy law down to our imperfect level. By saying that man cannot keep God's law perfectly, we establish its perfection and holiness. Listen to Paul in Romans 3:28,

> Therefore we conclude that a man is justified by faith without the deeds of the law (Rom. 3:28).

WITHOUT THE DEEDS OF THE LAW. Paul anticipates the accusation that he was trying to discredit the law and asks the question,

Do we then make void the law? (Rom. 3:31).

Paul says that (these are not my words), and Paul also answers as follows:

. . . God forbid: yea, we establish the law (Rom. 3:31).

To say that I by myself cannot keep the law of God perfectly is an admission of the holiness, the perfection, the righteousness of that law. I confess that the law is so high, so good, so holy, that I, a poor, weak, depraved sinner cannot in myself meet its high and holy demands. I extoll the holiness of the law and exalt it; I establish the law by admitting my inability to keep it and turning from the law I flee to Christ for mercy, for pardon, for grace, and say:

> Nothing in my hands I bring,
>   Simply to the Cross I cling.
> Not the labor of my hands,
>   Could fulfil Thy law's demand.
>
> Could my zeal no respite know,
>   Could my tears forever flow.
> These for sin could not atone.
>   Thou must save, and Thou alone.

That, beloved, is Bible salvation. Oh, sinner, turn from your labors of works to Christ, for grace. Do you want to be saved? Then stop trying, and try trusting!

Chapter Ten

THE FAITH OF ABRAHAM

> Even as Abraham believed God, and it was accounted
> to him for righteousness (Gal. 3:6).

THE Epistle of Paul to the Galatian churches was
written to correct a serious error. Paul had taught that
salvation was by the grace of God, and that we are also
kept by the grace of God. But certain false teachers had
come who denied this Gospel of grace. They insisted
that while saved by grace, we are then kept by our own
works. As a result these Galatians had lost their assurance
and gone back to the bondage of the law. This called
forth Paul's severe rebuke in chapter 3.

> O foolish Galatians, who hath bewitched you....
> Are ye so foolish? having BEGUN in the Spirit, are ye now
> made perfect by the flesh (the works of the flesh)?
> He therefore that ministereth to you the Spirit, and
> worketh miracles among you, doeth he it by the works
> of the law, or by the hearing of faith? (Gal. 3:1, 3, 5).

EXAMPLE OF ABRAHAM

To prove that we are not saved or kept by the works
of the law, Paul then refers them to the history of Abraham. How was Abraham saved? How was Abraham kept?
By the Law? Impossible, for Abraham knew nothing
about the Law. He lived four hundred years before the
law was given (Gal. 3:17). How then was Abraham saved
and kept? Here is Paul's answer:

> Even as Abraham believed God, and it was accounted
> to him for righteousness (Gal. 3:6).

Abraham believed God. This is also stated in Romans 4:3. Here Paul asserts:

> ... Abraham believed God, and it was counted unto him for righteousness (Rom. 4:3).

Notice that in both passages (Gal. 3:6 and Rom. 4:3) it is said that Abraham "believed God." It does not say that he believed IN GOD, but he BELIEVED GOD. There is an infinity of difference between believing IN God and believing God. Even the devils believe IN God. Only the fool says "there is no God" (Ps. 14:1). A man may believe IN God, but unless he BELIEVES GOD, he is still lost. To believe God is to accept HIS WORD, to TRUST HIS PROMISE. Just believing in the existence of God is not enough. We must believe what He says. The only book which contains His promises is the Bible, so that believing God is believing HIS WORD. Abraham believed what God said. Therefore, the vital question is: "What did Abraham believe?" We have the answer given in Genesis 15, from which Paul quotes in our text. Genesis 15 is the great faith chapter of the Old Testament, just as Hebrews 11 is of the New Testament. In the record of Abraham we have the complete story of the Gospel. This is the claim of Paul in Galatians 3:8,

> And the scripture, foreseeing that God would justify the heathen through faith, preached before the gospel unto Abraham, saying, In thee shall all nations be blessed (Gal. 3:8).

THE GOSPEL TO ABRAHAM

The Gospel that God preached to Abraham centers about a promised son, Isaac; his birth, his death, and his resurrection. Isaac was a type of Jesus. He was a picture of His virgin birth, a picture of His death when Abraham took him to Mt. Moriah, and a picture of Christ in His resurrection when God called to Abraham to spare his son. We turn to Genesis for the record of this Gospel. Genesis 15 opens with:

> After these things the word of the Lord came unto Abram in a vision, saying, Fear not, Abram: I am thy shield, and thy exceeding great reward (Gen. 15:1).

Abram had just returned from his great victory over the four kings of the north, and he had delivered Lot and his family and the five other kings. Now he becomes afraid, and fears that the kings against whom he fought will come back for revenge later on. Moreover, he had refused to take any of the spoil, and this too may have troubled him. It is then that the Lord comes to encourage him, and says, "Fear not, Abram: I am thy shield." That is, "Don't be afraid, Abram, for I will be your protector." Then the Lord adds, "and thy exceeding great reward." God seems to say, "You have refused the wealth of the spoils of the king of Sodom, but I Myself will be your reward."

To this promise of God, Abram made a strange reply. He tells God he is not so sure that he can believe God, since another promise God had made previously to him had not yet been fulfilled. It was the promise which God had made many, many years before, and which up until now He had not fulfilled. God had promised Abram a son by Sarai his wife. The years had slipped by, and it was now thirty years since God had promised this son whom Abram desired so much. Abram therefore reminds God of this and says:

> ... Lord God, what wilt thou give me, seeing I go childless, and the steward of my house is this Eliezer of Damascus?

> And Abram said, Behold, to me thou hast given no seed:
> and, lo, one born in my house is mine heir (Gen. 15:2, 3).

Abram complains bitterly that the promise of a seed
has not been kept. But the Lord immediately reassures
Abram, saying:

> ... This shall not be thine heir; but he that shall come
> forth out of thine own bowels shall be thine heir.
>
> And he brought him forth abroad, and said, Look now
> toward heaven, and tell the stars, if thou be able to number
> them: and he said unto him, So shall thy seed be.
>
> And he believed in the Lord; and he counted it to him
> for righteousness (Gen. 15:4-6).

What Did Abram Believe?

Now what did God ask Abram to believe? He asked
him to believe what He had said concerning a promised
son. But more than that, God asked him to believe in
a long-promised son, a long-delayed son, a miraculously
born, a supernaturally given, son. God asked Abram
to believe the humanly impossible, the naturally un-
reasonable and the miraculously supernatural. When
God repeated this promise to Abram he was one hundred
years old, and his wife Sarai was ninety. They had both
long since passed the time of life when they, in the
ordinary course of nature, could expect to become parents
of a child. Abram's body was "dead" we are told, as far
as procreation was concerned. Sarai had long since passed
the time of life for childbearing, and was maternally
dead. It would therefore take a miracle to give them
a child. It would have to be supernatural.

Sarah and Abraham Were Dead

In Genesis 18:11 we read this:

> Now Abraham and Sarah were old and well stricken in
> age; and it ceased to be with Sarah after the manner of
> women.

Abraham and Sarah were old and well stricken in years. That means that they were decrepit, senile, tottering in their old age. Sarah had long since passed the age of childbearing, for we read in God's Word, that "it ceased to be with Sarah after the manner of women" (Gen. 18:11). In Hebrews 11:11 we read:

> Through faith also Sara herself received strength to conceive seed, and was delivered of a child when she was past age, because she judged him faithful who had promised.

What was true of Sarah was true of Abraham also. He too had passed the years of fertility, and was sexually impotent to produce a child in the usual course of nature. The verses we quoted include Abraham as being old and well stricken in years; and referring again to our opening Scripture in Romans 4, we gain the following interesting information. Speaking of Abraham, Paul says in Romans 4:18-22:

> Who against hope believed in hope, that he might become the father of many nations, according to that which was spoken, So shall thy seed be.
> And being not weak in faith, he considered not his own body now dead, when he was about an hundred years old, neither yet the deadness of Sarah's womb:
> He staggered not at the promise of God through unbelief; but was strong in faith, giving glory to God;
> And being fully persuaded that, what he had promised, he was able also to perform.
> And therefore it was imputed to him for righteousness.

Here then is the divine record itself. Abraham's body was dead; Sarah's womb was dead. Unless a miracle happened, they could have no children. But God still promised a son and Abraham believed God's promise, even though it meant a miracle: and this faith saved him. The birth of Isaac was as great a miracle as the virgin

birth of the Lord Jesus Christ, of whom he was only
a type. Abraham believed God's Word concerning this
son, and it was imputed unto him for righteousness.

FOR US ALSO

What was true of Abraham is true today. Salvation and
justification still come by believing God's Word concerning His Son, His miraculously conceived, supernaturally
born, Son. That is what John says in I John 5:9, 10,

> If we receive the witness of men, the witness of God is
> greater: for this is the witness of God which he hath
> testified of his Son.
> He that believeth on the Son of God hath the witness
> in himself: he that believeth not God hath made him
> a liar; because he believeth not the record that God gave
> of his Son (I John 5:9, 10).

The truth here is as clear as it can be stated: salvation
is believing what God says about His Son Jesus Christ.
God knows of no other way of redemption for lost
humanity.

Therefore, the all-important question is: Have you
believed on the Son of God? If you have, then you are
saved. If you have not, then you are still in your sin.
What is needed is not reason, not feeling, not emotion,
but faith. Moreover, Abraham received no visions,
emotions, or fleshly sensation, nothing but the promise
of God in His Word. And this is God's way of salvation,
for Paul ends the chapter on Abraham's faith in his
Epistle to the Romans with these important words:

> Now it was not written for his (that is, Abraham's) sake
> alone, that it was imputed to him;
> But for us also, to whom it shall be imputed, if we believe
> on him that raised up Jesus our Lord from the dead;
> Who was delivered for our offences, and was raised again
> for our justification (Rom. 4:23-25).

Chapter Eleven

ABRAHAM'S CHILDREN

... Abraham believed God, and it was counted unto him for righteousness (Rom. 4:3).

Know ye therefore that they which are of faith, the same are the children of Abraham (Gal. 3:7).

THE burden of the Epistle to the Galatians is the place of the law of God in salvation. Paul had stated again and again that if salvation depends even in the least bit upon our works, then the sacrifice of Christ becomes the most colossal mistake of eternity. If there were one man who could be saved by his own efforts, or works of the law, then the death of Christ was unnecessary. He sums it up in Galatians 2:21,

... if righteousness come by the law, then Christ is dead in vain (Gal. 2:21).

In the light of this, Paul is amazed at the foolishness of these Galatians, who after having experienced deliverance from the curse of the law, would go back again under its bondage.

Are ye so foolish? having begun in the Spirit, are ye now made perfect by the flesh? (Gal. 3:3).

ENTER ABRAHAM

To illustrate his point, the apostle introduces Abraham. How was he saved? By believing what God said about a long-promised, supernaturally born son. He believed the Gospel (Gal. 3:8). The Gospel is the good news of the death and resurrection of this virgin-born Son of

93

promise. Abraham also believed God's Word concerning
the miraculous birth of Isaac. When Isaac was full grown,
God commanded Abraham to take this miraculously born
son to a mountain to sacrifice him on an altar. The story
is in Genesis 22, and is one of the most complete pictures
of the Gospel, of the death and resurrection of the virgin-
born Son of God. Abraham obeys God, and takes his son
Isaac, and there "potentially" puts him to death. In God's
eyes, Isaac was sacrificed, for God accepted the MOTIVE
for the ACT. Abraham believed he would actually have
to kill his son. For three days, Isaac was therefore potentially dead in the experience of Abraham. The writer of
Hebrews confirms this:

> By faith Abraham, when he was tried, offered up Isaac
> (Heb. 11:17a).

And the next part says:

> ... and he that had received the promises offered up
> his only begotten son (Heb. 11:17b).

Abraham actually offered up his son in the sight of
God. It only means this: as far as Abraham was concerned, Isaac was really dead. When Abraham started
out on the journey early in the morning, he had no other
idea than that God meant what He said, and that he
must, after three days, put Isaac to death on Mt. Moriah.
For three days he considered his son Isaac dead—potentially dead. So Isaac becomes a wonderful type of the
Lord Jesus Christ in His death, for three days and three
nights. Then follows the resurrection.

In Genesis 22, verse 13, we read:

> And Abraham lifted up his eyes, and looked, and behold
> behind him a ram caught in a thicket by his horns: and
> Abraham went and took the ram, and offered him up for
> a burnt-offering in the stead of his son (Gen. 22:13).

Isaac has been dead in the mind of Abraham for three days, and now all of a sudden he is returned to life. That is resurrection. Isaac had been considered dead for three days, but now God says, "Take the ram, and let Isaac live." That is resurrection. When we turn to Hebrews 11:17-19 we read this:

> By faith Abraham, when he was tried, offered up Isaac: and he that had received the promises offered up his only begotten son.
> Of whom it was said, That in Isaac shall thy seed be called:
> Accounting that God was able to raise him up, even from the dead; from whence also he received him in a figure (Heb. 11:17-19).

Abraham knew and believed all the time that God was going to do something miraculous. He knew God promised that Isaac would be the father of the covenant nation, but now he was to die. How then can God keep His promise? There was only one way out. In order to keep His promise, God would have to raise up Isaac from the dead. That is all. There was only one way for God to keep His Word under these circumstances, and that was to raise him up again; and after three days he was raised up from the dead in type and in figure, and the joy of resurrection was seen upon the mountain where the Son of God was to be slain.

ONLY ONE WAY

Abraham believed in the death and the resurrection of his son. That is the Gospel; and undoubtedly that is what Paul referred to when he says "that the gospel was before preached) unto Abraham."

And today this Gospel is still the same. As Abraham was saved by believing what God said concerning a miraculously born son, his death and resurrection, so we must believe God's record of His Son of whom Isaac was the type. Abraham is the example of saving faith, and therefore is called the Father of the faithful, and believers are called the children of Abraham.

> Know ye therefore that they which are of faith, the same are the children of Abraham (Gal. 3:7).

Again Paul says at the close of his reference to Abraham:

> So then they which be of faith are blessed with faithful Abraham (Gal. 3:9).

We are not children of Abraham by natural birth, but by personal faith in the Word of God. Abraham's faith is our example. The Apostle Paul in commenting on the verse, "Abraham believed God, and it was counted unto him for righteousness" (Rom. 4:3), concludes the argument as follows:

> Now it was not written for his (Abraham's) sake alone, that it was imputed to him;
> But for us also, to whom it shall be imputed, if we believe on him that raised up Jesus our Lord from the dead;
> Who was delivered for our offences, and raised again for our justification (Rom. 4:23-25).

To this the Apostle John bears witness when he says concerning faith in God's Word as the only ground of salvation:

> If we receive the witness of men, the witness of God is greater: for this is the witness of God which he hath testified of his Son.
> He that believeth on the Son of God hath the witness in himself: (The witness of the Spirit is the Word of God. If you believe that, you have the witness within yourself.) he that believeth not God hath made him a liar; because he believeth not the RECORD that God gave of his Son (I John 5:9, 10).

God's Witness

The witness of the Spirit is not some wonderful feeling, some great sense of exhilaration. It is not voices from heaven, or visions, or sensations, dreams or emotions. The witness is God's Word, and when we believe it, we have the witness. This will result in joy and peace and may well be accompanied by great emotional responses or even happy dreams, but these are the RESULT of believing the TESTIMONY OF THE SPIRIT IN THE WORD OF GOD—believing the record God has given of His Son.

What more can a believer ask than the PROMISE of God? To ask for additional evidence is to insult God. To ask for additional evidence is an admission that God's Word alone is not enough. Beloved, your feelings are subject to change, but God's Word never changes. To depend upon emotions and feelings is a miserable experience. Even when I feel I am lost, I can still turn to the WORD OF GOD for my assurance. After asserting the fact that our salvation is wholly of faith, and illustrating it by the example of Abraham, Paul concludes his argument by one of the strongest statements in the entire epistle, a statement we take up in detail later but which we quote now:

> For as many as are of the works of the law are under the curse: for it is written, Cursed is every one that continueth not in all things which are written in the book of the law to do them (Gal. 3:10).

Can we be saved by the works of the law? Positively not! for "by the works of the law shall no flesh be justified in his sight." Someone will say, "But after we are saved, then surely we can be kept by the law." Absolutely not! for it calls for CONTINUED, UNBROKEN perfect

obedience in every single point. One slip and you are
guilty. Is there a saint who can say that he has ever lived
one day without breaking God's law? Have you ever
lived one day without having an evil thought, speaking
one hasty word, wasting one precious moment, one second
in which you thought or spoke ill of a brother? One
day in which you did not gossip or listen to gossip, one
day in which you felt no bitterness or resentment toward
your enemies? One day in which not a single foolish
thought entered your mind? Remember, the Bible says,
"The thought of foolishness is sin" (Prov. 24:9). Have
you neglected to speak for Christ on just one occasion?
Then you are guilty, and if you are under the law, you
are cursed the moment you fail.

No dodging now. Have you ever, since you were saved
by grace, failed once, only once, "to continue in all things
written in the book of the law to do them"? Then if you
are under law, you are under the curse. No wonder Paul
continues:

> But that no man is justified by the law in the sight of
> God, it is evident: for, The just shall live by faith.
> And the law is not of faith: but, The man that doeth
> them shall live in them (Gal. 3:11, 12).

Our only hope is in looking to Christ and His grace.
It is: saved by grace—kept by grace—and taught by grace
that:

> ... denying ungodliness and worldly lusts, we should
> live soberly, righteously, and godly, in this present world
> (Titus 2:12).

And:

> ... kept by the power of God through faith unto sal-
> vation ready to be revealed in the last time (I Pet. 1:5).

Chapter Twelve

THE CURSE OF THE LAW

> For as many as are of the works of the law are under the curse: for it is written, Cursed is every one that continueth not in all things which are written in the book of the law to do them (Gal. 3:10).

IN these unmistakable words of the Holy Spirit, Paul asserts that any man who at any time, or in any measure has ever broken one of the laws of God, only once, is under the curse of the law and is lost, condemned and hopeless as far as the penalty of the law is concerned. It is well to ponder these words carefully, and to ask yourself the question, "Am I under the law?" Then if you have not kept the entire law in every detail all of your life without a single interruption, then according to these unmistakable words, you are under the curse of God and must suffer the penalty of the law which is eternal death and separation from the presence of your Creator.

The Bible further states that no man lives, and that no man has ever lived (except Jesus), who has been able to keep the law of God perfectly. One single unclean thought, one hasty word, one little lie, one moment in life when we failed to love God with all our might and heart and strength makes us guilty of breaking God's law. Solomon says, "The thought of foolishness is sin." Well, you say then, all must be guilty. Exactly! That is exactly what God also says, "All have sinned and come short of the glory of God." In Psalm 14 David tells us this:

> The LORD looked down from heaven upon the children of men to see if there were any that did understand, and seek God (Ps. 14:2).

Here in the next verse is what God has to say that He found as He looked for those who sought after Him. Here is God's answer to the question:

> They are all gone aside, they are all together become filthy: there is none that doeth good, NO, NOT ONE (Ps. 14:3).

That, my friend, is God's verdict of every man by nature and by his first birth. That applies to you and to me, for He says that they are "all gone aside" and are filthy in God's sight. "There is none righteous, no, not one." God's perfect law condemns us one and all.

No, Not One

These are God's infallible words. If you want still more detail, read carefully the first three chapters of Romans, ending with God's verdict in verse 23:

> For all have sinned, and come short of the glory of God (Rom. 3:23).

Now let us turn back for a moment to the law of God. Upon all such this law pronounces a curse. The law can only bless the perfect. It must curse all the rest. You see, therefore, my friend, that brings all of us, each and every one of us, under the judgment of God and under the curse of the law. This leaves us hopeless and helpless in ourselves. We are guilty, and the law which is holy, and therefore cannot lie, MUST condemn the sinner with eternal death. If, therefore, God had given us only His perfect law, we would all necessarily be lost, we should all be destined to an eternal Hell.

GRACE ENTERS

But here God enters in with His wonderful message of grace. The law could not save, justify, or sanctify the sinner. It cannot make the sinner a saint, it cannot forgive sin, it cannot change the heart, it cannot teach us to live better, it cannot help us out of our predicament in any way whatsoever. All the law can do is demand punishment and justice, and pronounce our sentence, reveal our filthiness and unworthiness, and curse our disobedience with eternal death. That is the sole ministry of the law. It was never intended to save. God knew when He gave the law it would never save a single sinner, never make a single man better. He knew that no sinner would ever keep, yea, more than that, God knew that the very people He commanded to keep that law—could not in themselves keep it at all.

WHY THEN THE LAW?

But you ask then immediately: Is the law completely powerless? Can it do nothing at all? No, the law is not powerless. Its power is to reveal how sinful we are, and its power is to curse us for our sins. Indeed, the law is exceedingly powerful! But the law is utterly powerless to save a sinner or to sanctify the saint. That was never the purpose of the law. If it could have done that, Jesus would never have had to die at all, for then man could have been saved by his own works, and by the keeping of the law; and so Paul says in Romans 8:3,

> For what the law could not do, in that it was weak through the flesh, God sending his own Son in the likeness of sinful flesh, and for sin, condemned sin in the flesh (Rom. 8:3).

Will you please notice the first phrase of that verse! "For what the law COULD NOT DO!" There are some things then the law cannot do, and God never expected it to do. We ask, therefore, what was it? It could not justify, it could not save or pardon or redeem or improve or fix up or help or assist, forgive, or change the heart of the sinner. Now this is not a fault or weakness of the law, but, on the contrary, because of the strength of the law, and the weakness of the human flesh and heart. And so Paul adds after he says, "For what the law could not do—IN THAT IT WAS WEAK THROUGH THE FLESH." It was the weakness of the flesh which prevented the law from doing anything but cursing the sinner. The sinner's flesh is corrupt, even the saint's flesh is filthy and corrupt, and because the law is holy and perfect and just, it can only condemn such who have not kept the law.

What Then Is Our Hope?

Now comes a glorious revelation. What the law COULD NOT DO, the Lord Jesus Christ DID DO. He came to deliver us from the curse of the law. Yes, Jesus came to deliver us from the law itself. The law was a slave-driver, an executioner, seeking to kill us because of our sins. Then Jesus comes and does two things: first, He lives a perfect, holy, sinless life for thirty-three and one-half years in full, complete and perfect obedience to the law of God in every detail. He thereby provided a righteousness, a positive righteousness of the law. Then He did the second thing: He paid the death penalty of the law for us when He died on Calvary, and proved that He had paid it all by rising from the grave after three days. The penalty of the law was paid at Calvary, and, in addition, He has provided a perfect righteousness by His sinless life which is imputed to those that believe on Him. Now the Lord Jesus Christ offers both of these by grace, through faith, to any sinner who will turn from

Law to Grace, from his own works to Christ's work, and
be saved. To every sinner who will admit that he could
not keep the law of God and will receive the Lord Jesus
Christ, He does two things:

First, He imputes His death and resurrection to that
sinner. The law is satisfied in Christ, it has exacted its
full penalty in Him, and this payment is accounted to
the sinner. He now is a redeemed sinner whose debt
has been fully paid.

Second, Jesus, now imputes to this forgiven sinner
His perfect, sinless righteousness which He proved and
provided by His own sinless life, in perfect harmony with
the law, and now the believing sinner is clothed with the
righteousness of Christ Himself. By the death of the
Lord Jesus, the believer has had paid for him the penalty
of the law which he owed. By the life of the Lord Jesus
Christ he is now clothed with the perfect, sinless righteousness of Christ Himself, and stands before God as
though he had never committed a single sin in all his
life, and had never even once broken the holy law of God.
That, my friend, is justification, a truth which so few
seem to understand. The saint is not a pardoned sinner,
for the law knows no pardon. It knows no mercy. It
knows only punishment, and that is what Paul says in
Romans 8:

> For what the law could not do, in that it was weak
> through the flesh, God sending his own Son in the likeness
> of sinful flesh, and for sin, condemned sin in the flesh:
> That the righteousness of the law might be fulfilled in
> us, who walk not after the flesh, but after the Spirit (Rom.
> 8:3, 4).

Will you please notice that statement, "that the righteousness of the law might be fulfilled in us." It does
not say that the righteousness of the law might be ful-

filled BY us, but rather, IN us. And the Lord Jesus Christ does that. The righteousness of the law to which we could not attain, and which could not be fulfilled BY us, is provided by Him who bore our sins on Calvary in our stead. And so, coming back to our opening Scripture, Galatians 3:10, we remind you again of Paul's words:

> For as many as are of the works of the law are under the curse: for it is written, Cursed is every one that continueth not in all things which are written in the book of the law to do them (Gal. 3:10).

That is what the law demanded! Hopeless, helpless, condemned, vile, filthy, guilty before God we stand; but what the law could not do, Jesus did, and so we read in Galatians 3:13,

> Christ hath redeemed us from the curse of the law, being made a curse for us: for it is written, Cursed is every one that hangeth on a tree (Gal. 3:13).

Not under the Law

And now we are delivered, we have been discharged forever, from the law (Rom. 7:6). The law cannot condemn twice. The believer then is through with the law forever. He is delivered from the law, he is dead to the law (Gal. 2:19), and free from the law (Rom. 8:2). Oh, Christian, rejoice in this wonderful salvation and this marvelous redemption provided by the Lord Jesus Christ. May I repeat again:

> . . . Cursed is every one that continueth not in all things which are written in the book of the law to do them (Gal. 3:10b).

It is not a matter of keeping the law partly, it is not a matter of living a holy life for a short time, but the Scripture says, "Cursed is every one that continueth not." It must be an uninterrupted, unbroken obedience to the law of God if we ever hope to find salvation by our own efforts and by our own works.

I do want to bring a very definite appeal to those of you who are still without the Lord Jesus Christ, and are hoping to attain Heaven and salvation without coming and believing on Him as your own personal Saviour. There are so many today who believe that if they live a good life, and join a church, and go through all the rituals of religion, and behave themselves, and make an honest effort to keep the law to the best of their ability, that then God will save them. The Bible knows nothing of this kind of a salvation. God says, "There is none that doeth good, no not one." We have all gone astray, we are together become unprofitable. And for this very reason the Lord Jesus Christ had to die on the Cross of Calvary to provide that which we ourselves were absolutely unable to attain. The law was not intended to save, but rather to show us our need of salvation. It is, according to Paul, a schoolmaster, to teach us the lesson of our own inability, and so to make us ready to receive the free gift of God by His own wonderful grace. Someone has compared the law to a mirror, in which we can see how soiled our face is, but it has no power to cleanse, and so we turn from the mirror after we have seen the awful condition of our own filthiness, to Him who alone by His own precious blood can redeem us and wash us from our sins. And then, when you have received Him, God gives you the assurance that the law has been fulfilled by Christ. His righteousness is imputed to you, His penalty which He paid is now your payment of sin, and you can say with us:

> Free from the law, Oh, happy condition!
> Jesus has died and there is remission.

Cursed by the law, and ruined by the fall,
Christ hath redeemed us, once for all.

Once for all, oh, doubter believe it,
One for all, oh, sinner, receive it.
Come to the Cross, your burden will fall,
Christ hath redeemed us, once for all.

Chapter Thirteen

REDEEMED FROM THE CURSE

Christ hath redeemed us from the curse of the law, being made a curse for us: for it is written, Cursed is every one that hangeth on a tree:

That the blessing of Abraham might come on the Gentiles through Jesus Christ; that we might receive the promise of the Spirit through faith.

Brethren, I speak after the manner of men; Though it be but a man's covenant, yet if it be confirmed, no man disannulleth, or addeth thereto (Gal. 3:13-15).

WHEN God gave the Law on the tables of stone on Mount Sinai, He knew that no human being could keep that Holy Law. Yea, He knew that no one ever would. Nay, more, God never expected a single sinner to keep His Law. That was not the purpose of the Law. God gave the Law to PROVE that man could not be saved by LAW WORKS, in order that it might convince all mankind of the need of the grace of God and get them ready to accept the mercy of God in Christ Jesus. The Law is perfect; that is why imperfect men cannot keep it. The Law is holy; that is why sinners are condemned by it. The Law is just, and therefore cannot show mercy to the guilty, for that would be in violation of its justness. The Law is holy; that is why sinners are condemned by demns and says, "Cursed is every one that continueth not in ALL THINGS written in the law to do them."

Redeemed by Christ

Now notice Galatians 3:13,

> Christ hath redeemed us from the curse of the law, being made a curse for us (Gal. 3:13).

Christ hath redeemed us from THE CURSE of the Law. The CURSE of the Law is the penalty of the LAW, even death. Christ by His death hath delivered us from ETERNAL DEATH, the penalty of a broken Law. A law without penalties is powerless. The only thing which makes a law something to be feared is the fact that it demands punishment. If the Law cannot punish, that is, if the penalty, the curse, is gone, it cannot touch the transgressor any more. That is what legislators mean when they say, PUTTING TEETH IN THE LAW, making the penalty so severe that men will be forced to keep it. But when the penalty is removed the teeth are taken out. To every believer, then, the penalty of the Law has been met by the Saviour. He bore our sins in His own body on the tree. Jesus said:

> He that heareth my word, and believeth on him that sent me, hath everlasting life, and shall not come into condemnation; but is passed from death unto life (John 5:24).

To accept Christ is to be free from the Law with its curse and its condemnation. To accept Christ is to have ETERNAL LIFE.

The Great Question

And right here we must once more answer an inescapable question. If we are saved by grace and kept by grace, does not this gender carelessness and looseness of living? If the believer is secure and cannot again be lost, can he then do anything he wants to and not suffer the penalty? Of course not! It is not a question of penalty, but a question of God's faithfulness. The fact that God will not forsake the believer does not mean that he is not responsible to God for all his conduct. The person who makes the grace of God an excuse for sinning, either has never been born again, or he does not understand grace. God has made provision for the saint who slips and falls, and says:

> If we confess our sins, he is faithful and just to forgive us our sins, and to cleanse us from all unrighteousness (I John 1:9).

In the second chapter of this same epistle, John says:

> My little children, these things write I unto you, that ye sin not. And if any man sin, we have an advocate with the Father, Jesus Christ the righteous:
> And he is the propitiation for our sins: and not for our's only, but also for the sins of the whole world (I John 2:1, 2).

In Galatians 6:1 we are told,

> ... if a man be overtaken in a fault, ye which are spiritual, restore such an one in the spirit of meekness; considering thyself, lest thou also be tempted (Gal. 6:1).

Perfect forgiveness is provided for the repentant believer. But for wilful disobedience, making the grace of God an excuse for sin, God deals very differently. The Lord will not overlook sin in the life of a believer. Failure to confess our sin and FORSAKE it calls for the judgment of God. The words to the believer are unmistakable:

> For if we sin WILFULLY after that we have received the knowledge of the truth, there remaineth no more sacrifice for sins,
> But a certain fearful looking for of judgment and fiery indignation (Heb. 10:26, 27).

WEAKNESS AND SICKNESS

Paul in writing to the carnal Corinthians says that

those who refuse to acknowledge and judge sin in their own lives, will be visited by God's judgment and chastening. This may take the form of physical chastening. He says in I Corinthians 11:30,

> For this cause many are weak and sickly among you, and many sleep.
> For if we would judge ourselves, we should not be judged (I Cor. 11:30, 31).

Don't ever imagine that a believer can make the grace of God an occasion for careless living. If you say, "Let us sin that grace may abound," you are inviting the judgment of God. Sooner or later God will send weakness, sickness and chastening. If still persisted in, God may step in and send death to put an end to His child's rebellion and his mistaken notion that he can escape God's dealing in the severest way with him. Yes, the Lord will judge His people!

There is only one way to escape this judgment upon a believer's sin. It is self-judgment, confession and forsaking of the sin. But having said all this, we must emphasize that this judgment of God upon a believer's sin does NOT IN ANY WAY AFFECT HIS SALVATION, because that depends upon grace, and not upon behavior. Our position in Christ depends upon God's faithfulness. Our enjoyment, assurance, blessing and rewards rest upon OUR faithfulness. This was the truth Paul wanted to drive home to these Galatians.

GOD AND ISRAEL

To illustrate this great fact of our unbreakable union with Christ, He goes once more to the history of Abraham. Notice the 17th verse of Galatians 3. Paul illustrates in this verse the fact that ONCE under the grace of God, the Law has no more dominion. He takes first the

covenant of grace to Abraham and then the Law of God
through Moses 430 years later. The fact that Israel failed
under the Law does not annul God's covenant of grace
made before with Abraham. Notice the words:

> And this I say, that the covenant, that was confirmed
> before of God in Christ, the law, which was four hundred
> and thirty years after, cannot disannul, that it should make
> the promise of none effect.
>
> For if the inheritance be of the law, it is no more of
> promise: but God gave it to Abraham by promise (Gal.
> 3:17, 18).

Paul uses the Nation of Israel as an example. Israel
as a nation was under God's covenant of grace. They still
are and ever will be, for God's covenant which He swore
by HIMSELF cannot be broken. The fact that Abraham's seed (Israel) BROKE HIS LAW, and brought
upon them God's discipline, does not, however, annul
God's covenant of grace. All this is given as an illustration
for us. If we are saved, we are saved by grace, and grace
alone. Our salvation depends on what Jesus did; not
what WE do. It depends not on what we feel but what
JESUS felt for us. It depends not on OUR FAITHFUL-
NESS, but on His faithfulness. And as it was with Israel,
so it is with us. Disobedience will bring God's chastening,
but His covenant of grace still keeps us. God is faithful;
He cannot deny Himself. For the believer to be dis-
obedient is to invite God's disciplinary dealings. Israel
found it out for the past twenty-five hundred years. They
have been scattered out of the land because they broke
God's Law, but they are still God's covenant people, and
will once again be regathered and blessed. Our salvation
too depends on grace, but our enjoyment of this salvation
depends on our behavior. Our justification is by faith,
but our rewards will be by works. Your eternal life is

GOD'S GIFT and does not depend on anything you do.
It is all of grace.

To clinch this great truth Paul concludes the illustration of the covenant of grace with Abraham and his
seed, and the covenant of the law with Israel, in these
words:

> For if the inheritance (the land of Canaan) be of the
> law, it is no more of promise: but God gave it to Abraham
> by (unconditional) promise (Gal. 3:18).

THE MOTIVE FOR SERVICE

Our union with Christ is forever, but our communion
can be broken. This very fact that our union with Christ
cannot be broken, although our communion with Him
can be interrupted by sin in our lives, should constitute
the most powerful motive for a holy life of obedience.
The very fact that we are kept by grace, in spite of our
unworthiness should impel us to walk carefully and cir-
cumspectly. Grace should do far more than the Law
demands. Grace should be our teacher. Instead of grace
being an excuse for sin, it should be its great deterrent.

In Romans 6:1 Paul says:

> What shall we say then? Shall we continue in sin, that
> grace may abound? (Rom. 6:1).

Listen to Paul's answer to this charge:

> God forbid. How shall we that are dead to sin, live any
> longer therein? (Rom. 6:2).

Or listen to these words of Paul in Titus 2:11,

> For the grace of God that bringeth salvation hath ap-
> peared to all men,
> Teaching us that, denying ungodliness and worldly lusts,
> we should live soberly, righteously, and godly, in this present
> world (age) (Titus 2:11, 12).

The grace of God teaches true holiness. Would you

dare to substitute the word "law" for "grace" here in Titus 2:11 and read it like this:

> For the law of God teaches us that denying all ungodliness and worldly lusts, we should live soberly—

Some indeed would like to read it that way, but that is not the way Paul states it. He knew that he needed grace, and says, "The grace of God teaches us holiness." This the Law cannot do. It should be evident, therefore, that Grace does what the Law could not do.

The Law cannot save; the Law cannot keep. It is only Christ who is able to do that. The Law was given by God to prove once and for all that man could not save himself by works. It was given to show the utter depravity of the flesh and of human nature, and cause us to flee to Christ for mercy, not for justice; for forgiveness, not condemnation.

We constantly face the criticism that to say the Law cannot keep, is to debase the Law. Instead, we exalt it! The demands of the Law are so high, that it cannot be kept by sinful man. And because the sinner cannot keep God's Law, Jesus came to fulfil it for the believer. Some would accuse us of destroying the Law, and quote Matthew 5:17, 18—

> Think not that I am come to destroy the law, or the prophets: I am not come to destroy, but to fulfil.
> For verily I say unto you, Till heaven and earth pass, one jot or one tittle shall in no wise pass from the law, till all be fulfilled (Matt. 5:17, 18).

Jesus did not DESTROY the law, but He fulfilled it. When He arose, He proved that He had paid the death penalty of that Law. The Law has not failed—but man failed under the Law. The Law is still as perfect as ever, still as "just" as ever, and will condemn the sinner. The only hope lies in abandoning all hope of saving one's self, and casting one's self on the Grace of God, and God alone. We repeat, Jesus did not destroy the Law. It remains and ever will remain, the perfect demand of a righteous God for all who would save themselves. Since the sinner cannot keep it, the Law condemns him. But Christ fulfilled all its demands, and so while the Law is not dead, the believer is dead to the Law, and alive unto God.

Chapter Fourteen

WHY WAS THE LAW GIVEN?

> Wherefore then serveth the law? It was added because of transgressions, till the seed should come to whom the promise was made; and it was ordained by angels in the hand of a mediator (Gal. 3:19).

THE question in this verse is a natural one after the statements made by the Apostle Paul in the preceding verses. Paul anticipates in writing to the church that the question concerning the purpose of the law would be brought up, and so he answers the question before it could be asked. In the first three chapters of Galatians Paul had under the inspiration of the Holy Spirit proven that the Law of Moses was never given to make man better or to save him, much less to justify him. The law was given to condemn the sinner in order that he might realize the need of the grace of God. Paul had shown that the death of Christ is the final, conclusive argument that salvation cannot be by the law, for he says, "if righteousness come by the law then Christ is dead in vain." To teach salvation by the law is to deny both the necessity and the efficacy of the death of the Lord Jesus Christ. Neither can the law sanctify a man or make him better. All it could do was show him how bad he was, and how hopeless his condition without the grace of God.

WHY THEN THE LAW

And so Paul, having demonstrated that the law cannot

JUSTIFY or SANCTIFY or SATISFY the sinner or the saint, anticipates the question he knew men would ask, "Wherefore then serveth the law?" Then what is the law for, if it cannot save a man, or make him better, or keep him? To this question Paul gives the answer:

> ... It was added because of transgressions, till the seed should come.

Now three definite things are stated in this brief verse:

1. The law did have a beginning. Paul says "it was added"—added to something else which must have existed before the law itself came.

2. The law had a definite purpose, "because of transgressions," or as we shall see, to reveal the true nature of sin by transgression.

3. The law also came to an end, just as it had a beginning—"it was added—TILL the seed should come." It also came to an end when that seed did come.

Nowhere in Scripture is the purpose of the law more clearly stated than in this verse, and don't tell me that this applies only to the ceremonial or the dietary or the sanitary laws or the sacrifices of the Old Testament. Paul is speaking of THE LAW—the whole law, and the law of the Ten Commandments in particular. He is speaking of the law which cursed the sinner, even God's holy law. The clever distinction by some between the laws of Moses so-called, and the law of God, is without a single verse of support in the Bible, but is the invention of man himself, who would rather be condemned by the law than to be saved by the grace of God.

THE BEGINNING OF THE LAW

Now for a closer look at these things which Paul asserts in Galatians 3:19. Notice that three things are stated concerning the law. They are:

1. The beginning of the law.
2. The purpose of the law.
3. The end of the law.

First then, the law's beginning. When was the law added, and to what was it added? We call your attention first to the words of John the Baptist as he heralded the coming of the King of Kings, the Lord Jesus Christ. He says in John 1:17,

> For the law was given by Moses, but grace and truth came by Jesus Christ (John 1:17).

Nothing can be plainer than this verse. The law—the whole body of the law was given to Israel—was delivered by Moses as he received it direct from Almighty God. To this Paul evidently refers in Galatians 3:19, for the complete verse reads like this:

> Wherefore then serveth the law? It was added because of transgressions, till the seed should come to whom the promise was made; and it was ordained by angels in the hand of a mediator (Gal. 3:19).

Now that mediator as we all know, was Moses, the lawgiver. We can turn to the record in Exodus 20 and find all the details given under inspiration. But until God gave these Ten Commandments written upon tables of stone, Israel knew nothing about these laws as they are now given. For over two thousand years, from Adam to Moses, God gave no Ten Commandments to man. This is quite evident from Romans 5:13,

> For until the law sin was in the world: but sin is not imputed when there is no law (Rom. 5:13).

We shall deal with the last part of this verse more fully later on, but for now we would have you notice the first phrase, "until the law, sin was in the world." There was then a time when the law came, and therefore, before it came it did not exist in the form of written commandments. Next, please notice that there did exist something else, however, before the law came, and to which Paul says the law was added. Now when we add something, we of course imply and pre-suppose that there was something to which to add. To what then was the law added? Under what did men live before God gave the law by Moses? We all know the answer—it was the Grace of God. Adam was under grace, Noah was under grace, Abraham was under grace. God dealt in grace before the law, and during the law, and since the law. He still deals in grace. In Galatians 3, verse 8, we learn that the Gospel, "the good news," was preached already to Abraham. Now the Gospel is the good news to the sinner, that by grace through faith he may be saved, apart from the works of the law. But the law is not good news to the sinner. On the contrary, the law is very very bad news for the transgressor and the sinner, for the law tells this sinner and shows him how wicked he is; and he is accursed and condemned by this law, and therefore must be executed by the law, for his sins. Now this bad news of the law was added to the good news of grace. Notice, Paul says definitely, "it was added." It did not take the place of grace, it was not mixed with grace, it did not supplant the grace of God. It was added. Now the word "added" is "prostithemi" in the original Greek, and means "to place along side of." We may therefore say that the law came in and was placed along side of grace. It is important to notice this distinction. Grace was not removed when the law came in; it remained there for all who would see how utterly unworthy they were in the eyes of the law, and fleeing from the curse of the law would throw themselves upon the mercy and the grace of God alone. The Israelite under the law was saved by grace just as Abraham before the law, and just as we must be saved after the law.

NOT LAW AND GRACE

The law, therefore, was added to the gospel of grace to show and to reveal the awfulness and true character of sin, and the great need of the grace of God. By the works of the law no one was ever saved or ever can be. This is made clear in another question Paul raises by anticipation in verse 21. Here it is:

> Is the law then against the promises (the gospel) of God? God forbid: for if there had been a law given which could have given life, verily righteousness should have been by the law.
>
> But the scripture hath concluded all under sin, that the promise by faith of Jesus Christ might be given to them that BELIEVE (Gal. 3:21, 22).

If the law could have given life, says Paul, then Christ would never have needed to die. If a man can save himself, then why does he need a Saviour to die in his place? If a man can keep himself saved, then why does he need a High Priest to intercede daily for him at the right hand of God? No, indeed, says Paul, the law and the Gospel are not against each other, but they do have entirely different purposes. The law slays and kills the sinner, that he may turn from the law and his own works to the Christ who alone can give him life.

BEFORE THE LAW

Since the law was given by Moses, then there was a time when the law of Moses did not exist. If sin is only a transgression of the law, then there could have been no sin in the world before the law was given. But there was sin, for there was death. Before the law there could be

no transgression of the law, but sin is more than a transgression of the law. To be sure, Paul says in Romans 4:15,

> Because the law worketh wrath: for where no law is,
> there is no transgression (Rom. 4:15).

Notice carefully these inspired words through Paul,
"where no law is, there is no transgression." Before the
law came then, there could be no transgression of the
law. You ask immediately the question, "Was there no
sin then before the law came in?" Most assuredly, my
friend, there was sin, and sin was just as wicked and
just as horrible and just as terrible before the law as
it is since the law was given. There was sin before the
law, but no transgression. But man did not realize the
gravity and the awfulness of his sin, and for that very
purpose God gave the law in order that he might reveal
to man the awfulness of the sin which he was committing,
and of which he might even be unconscious. And so
God gave that law, and now the sin which had always
been morally wrong, becomes legally wrong; and in addition, the nature of transgression is given to sin. Transgression, after all, is only one aspect of sin. The word
"transgression" comes from two other words, "trans" and
"gresso," and means "to go beyond." The law then was
given to prove to man that sin is sin in all its awfulness.
In Romans 3:20 Paul says this:

> Therefore by the deeds of the law there shall no flesh
> be justified in his sight: for by the law is the KNOWL-
> EDGE OF SIN (Rom. 3:20).

Now the law did not produce sin, neither did it make
the sin worse, neither was the law itself sin; it entered
because of transgressions, to make "sin exceeding sinful,"
which means to show the exceeding sinfulness of the sin

they had been committing. This is what **Paul** says in Romans 5:20,

> Moreover the law entered, that the offence might abound (Rom. 5:20).

The law then revealed the true nature of sin, that we might flee to Almighty God for His grace. In addition to sin always having been morally wrong, the law now made it legally wrong. John tells us:

> Whosoever committeth sin transgresseth also the law: for sin is the transgression of the law (I John 3:4).

No verse in the Bible has been more abused and misunderstood than this one. It is constantly quoted by legalists as though sin were always a transgression, and the only sin is transgression, but there is one word which disperses this interpretation. It is the word, ALSO.

> Whosoever committeth sin transgresseth ALSO the law.

But sin is more than transgression. That is the legal definition. Transgression is the legal aspect of sin. But we have seen that before the law, there already was sin, but it was not reckoned as a transgression of the law, which had not yet been given. A thing may be morally wrong, and yet be legally right.

SLAVERY

Up to one hundred years ago it was perfectly legal to own slaves in the United States of America. You could own slaves, buy them, sell them, pay for them—much or little or nothing. It was no transgression of any law on our books. But then the law came and made it illegal to buy, to sell, to own a slave, and it was made punishable with severity; yet slavery is no more nor less morally wrong NOW than before the law was made, but where there is no law, there is no transgression.

Before World War I, it was not a transgression of the law to drink or to sell liquor and intoxicants, but during that war prohibition came in, making it a transgression of the law to sell, make, or buy intoxicants. Then the 18th amendment was repealed and it again became legal. The law against liquor was gone. Drinking was no more nor less morally wrong before or after that law, but the law made it a transgression at that time. Transgression of the law, therefore, is only one aspect of sin.

The Law Could Not Save

This then is the purpose of the law. It was not designed to save men or to make them better. Prohibition could forbid men drinking, but it could not stop them from thirsting and it blossomed out in an age of bootlegging, blind pigs, and wide-spread violations.

Why then the law of God, we ask again? The answer is, to reveal to man his utter corruption, his terrible sinfulness, that when Christ should come to save by grace, man would turn forever from the works of the law, and plead only the grace of God. The law was given to make sin exceeding sinful, a wilful rebellion against plain restrictions. The law increases your condemnation. Sinner, will you turn to Christ, abandon all hope of keeping the law for your salvation, and come to Him who said:

> Come unto me, all ye that labour and are heavy laden, and I will give you rest (Matt. 11:28).

Chapter Fifteen

GOD'S GREAT EXPERIMENT

> Wherefore then serveth the law? It was added because of
> transgressions, till the seed should come (Gal. 3:19).

SINCE the law cannot save a man or make a man better,
then why did God give the law in the first place? This
is the question which Paul anticipated. In dealing with
this question we shall see that it was:

1. Dispensational
2. National
3. Experimental
4. Demonstrational
5. Revelational
6. Impossible

The law had its beginning at Sinai and ended at
Calvary. There was a time when there was no written
law of Ten Commandments. There is no mistaking the
words of John:

> For the law was given by Moses, but grace and truth came
> by Jesus Christ (John 1:17).

In John 7:19 Jesus asks:

> Did not Moses give you the law, and yet none of you
> keepeth the law?

LAW WAS NATIONAL

Besides the dispensational character of the law, it was
also national, given to one definite nation, the Nation of
Israel. Paul establishes this beyond a shadow of doubt.

> For as many as have sinned without law shall also perish without law: and as many as have sinned in the law shall be judged by the law (Rom. 2:12).

Notice, will you, that there are two classes of people spoken of here: those who sinned WITHOUT LAW and those who sinned IN THE LAW. Who are they? The 14th verse of Romans 2 tells us:

> For when the GENTILES, WHICH HAVE NOT THE LAW, do by nature the things contained in the law, these, HAVING NOT THE LAW, are a law unto themselves (Rom. 2:14).

"For when the GENTILES, WHICH HAVE NOT THE LAW ..." Surely Scripture cannot be plainer. In Acts 15 this question of whether the Gentiles were under the Law of Moses came up at the first council at Jerusalem. And after the apostles had deliberated the point they sent this message back to the GENTILE CHRISTIANS at Antioch:

> Forasmuch as we have heard, that certain which went out from us have troubled you with words, subverting your souls, saying, Ye must be circumcised, and KEEP THE LAW: TO WHOM WE GAVE NO SUCH COMMANDMENT (Acts 15:24).

Peter in this same chapter accuses those who would put us under the law of "putting a yoke" on the shoulders of God's people which could not be borne. Listen to his words:

> Now therefore why tempt ye God, to put a yoke upon the neck of the disciples which neither our fathers nor we were able to bear?
> But WE BELIEVE that through the GRACE of the Lord Jesus Christ we shall be saved, even as they (Acts 15:10, 11).

God gave the law to this one nation as a demonstration of the inability of man to save himself by the law. It was, therefore, in addition to being dispensational and national, also experimental. This is clearly set forth in Romans 3:19,

> Now we know that what things soever the law saith, it saith to them who are under the law: that EVERY MOUTH may be stopped, and all the world may become guilty before God.
>
> Therefore by the deeds of the law there shall no flesh be justified in HIS SIGHT: for by the law is the KNOWLEDGE OF SIN (Rom. 3:19, 20).

God says that the LAW was given to Israel to stop the mouths of all men forever who would teach salvation by the law. God has tried that out on one whole nation for over fifteen hundred years and proven that it cannot be done. There is no need for further proof. For over fifteen hundred years God gave Israel the law as the perfect expression of His holy will, and after all those years not a single Jew had kept it. No one was saved by keeping that law, but every one who was saved was still saved BY FAITH and FAITH ALONE. And at the end of those years of law discipline, that nation ended up by nailing the ONLY MAN who ever did keep the law to the Cross of Calvary, to prove that fifteen hundred years of the LAW could not change the human heart, but only demonstrate how corrupt man is and how much he needs the grace of God. FOR BY THE LAW IS THE KNOWLEDGE OF SIN. Was the law at fault? Did the law fail? Ah, no! Man failed. The law did its work. It proved its perfection when imperfect men could not keep it. It proved it was not unjust, when it condemned the transgressor. When we say, therefore, that God never expected a single sinner to keep the law, we do not debase the law but exalt it. It was so perfect that it condemned the sinner. Do we make void the law? Nay, we establish the law. If we teach that man COULD keep the law, then we lower it to man's mean level. If ONE SINGLE PERSON could keep the law perfectly, there would be no need for the Cross of Christ, for "if righteousness come by the law, then Christ is dead in vain" (Gal. 2:21).

BANANAS IN CANADA

Let me illustrate. Imagine a man moving from Cuba to Canada. In Cuba he raised bananas successfully. He leases a tract of land in Canada and tells his landlord he is going to raise bananas. The landlord objects and says, "It cannot be done here," and the argument waxes hotter and hotter as one insists it can be done and the other KNOWS it cannot be done. Finally there is nothing left to do but permit the miguided farmer from Cuba to try it out. The boss helps him to make everything available for a good test, knowing beforehand it will not work. Now the whole farm of 640 acres is not planted, but only the most adaptable and naturally likely spot is chosen, say ten acres in the lee of a mountain, on the south exposure where the soil is the best. It is fertilized and thoroughly worked, the best of plants are procured, and all that summer the most meticulous care is bestowed upon the baby banana plants. But in late August comes a frost and the crop is a failure. They try it another year with the same result. And another, and another, and still another year, and always a frost and a failure. Now suppose they have tried it for FIFTEEN HUNDRED SEASONS. The owner finally says, "Now are you convinced?" No more testing is needed. By this experiment on the most likely soil under the most ideal conditions in all Canada it is proven that bananas WILL NOT GROW ANYWHERE IN CANADA. He has proven, not only that bananas cannot be grown on that particular ten acres, but NOWHERE ELSE IN CANADA, where the conditions are not even as good as they were here.

ISRAEL WAS GOD'S GARDEN

Israel thought that they could keep the law. No amount of dealing with them could convince them of the greatness of their sin. So God gave them a law; a perfect law, a holy law, a just law. Then He planted them in a sheltered land, drove out the enemies for them. He sent them godly priests and prophets and kings. He gave them a ritual and the oracles and a perfect law and said, "Now see what you can do." Under the most promising circumstances and blessings which no other nation ever enjoyed, He left them for fifteen hundred years under the law, but—NO BANANAS. God has now proven that NO ONE can be saved by the law, since the experiment of Israel under the most blessed and salutary conditions failed utterly and completely. Does God have to test it out on the rest of the world? Ah, no! He has proven that "by the works of the law there shall no flesh be justified in His sight, for by the law is the KNOWLEDGE of sin." Not salvation from sin, but the KNOWLEDGE OF SIN. Now I am sure you will the better understand Paul's words:

> Now we know that what things soever the law saith, it saith to them who are under the law: that every mouth may be stopped, and the whole world become guilty before God (Rom. 3:19).

And then, when Israel had proven themselves to be helpless, and by their failure had established the perfection and justice of God's law, Jesus came to show us the way of redemption. He paid the penalty of the broken law and suffered its condemnation and death and now offers to impute to every one who believes on Him, His own perfect righteousness by faith.

The law, therefore, was demonstrational. It demonstrated by the experiment of Israel "that no flesh could be justified by the deeds of the law in the sight of God." Paul says in Romans 7 that the law was added to make sin "exceeding sinful" by showing its true nature of rebellion against God.

This then was the ministry of the law, but this ministry ended at Calvary. Today the awfulness of sin can best be seen at Calvary instead of at Sinai. At Calvary we see the awfulness of sin, but also God's remedy for sin. The law could show us our danger, but it could not show us the way out. One glimpse of Calvary will do more to convict the sinner of his sin than all the thunderings of the law. For thirty-one years I attended church, and each Sunday heard the preacher solemnly read the Ten Commandments as a weekly ritual. For thirty-one years I heard the law, memorized it in both Dutch and English, but it did not bring conviction, until after all those years I came face to face one day with my sin AT CALVARY, and in five minutes I saw more of the horribleness of sin than I had seen under the law for almost a third of a century. I not only saw sin in all its lurid reality, but I also saw the cleansing blood, the blood that had to be sprinkled on the mercy seat in the Tabernacle over the broken law in the Ark of the covenant that called for justice and judgment and death, the blood of the sacrifice which was the only thing that could stand between a holy, righteous God and a broken law. I saw that blood and knew that it was shed for me, and I cried:

> Alas, and did my Saviour bleed?
> And did my Sovereign die?

Would He devote that sacred head,
    For such a worm as I?

Yes, it was for me the Saviour died,
    On Calvary's cruel tree.
There was the precious blood applied,
    From sin to set me free.

Look away from self today and look to Christ. Believe Him when He says, "Come unto me all ye that labour and are heavy laden, and I will give you rest" (Matt. 11:28). Stop trying, my friend, and TRY TRUSTING.

Rock of Ages, cleft for me,
    Let me hide myself IN THEE;
Let the water and the blood,
    From Thy wounded side which flowed,
Be of sin the double cure,
    Save from wrath and make me pure.

Not the labors of my hands,
    Could fulfill THY LAW'S DEMANDS;
Could my zeal no respite know,
    Could my tears forever flow,
These for sin could not atone;
    Thou must save, and Thou alone.

In my hands no price I bring,
    Simply to Thy Cross I cling.
Foul I to the fountain fly,
    WASH ME, Saviour, or I die.

Ho, every one that thirsteth, come ye to the waters, and he that hath no money; come ye, buy and eat; yea, come, buy wine and milk, without money, and without price.

Wherefore do ye spend money for that which is not bread? and your labour for that which satisfieth not? (Isa. 55:1, 2).

Chapter Sixteen

THE MOTIONS OF SINS

THE law, according to Paul in Galatians 3:19, began with Moses and was fulfilled in Christ. Its purpose was to demonstrate the need of grace in salvation. We have seen that it was, therefore:

1. Dispensational
2. National
3. Experimental
4. Demonstrational

We now come to another aspect of the law—its REVELATIONAL character. The law cast a light of awful revelation into fallen human nature. We turn to Romans 7:5,

> For when we were in the flesh, the motions of sins, which were by the law, did work in our members to bring forth fruit unto death (Rom. 7:5).

There is one phrase in this verse which is the key to its teaching. Notice particularly the words, "for the motions of sins, which were by the law." Now the motions of sins are the activities of sin, the movements of sin. These, said Paul, were by the law. Sin was not caused by the law, but sin was put in motion by the law. The law brought the sin to light, but it could not take it away. In verse 8 we read that "without the law sin was dead," dead in the sense of being quiet and motionless. Sin was there, but it seemed dead, and then the law came to stir up that which had been there all the time, but man was not conscious of it, for "by the law is the knowledge of sin." Let me illustrate. Imagine that I have before me a glass of water. It has been undisturbed for several hours or days. It has not been stirred or agitated at all; in other words, it is "dead water." It looks pretty good, it is clear and sparkling and looks good enough to drink. Except on very close inspection, you would never detect the fine layer of sediment in the bottom of the glass where it has settled, because the water was dead and undisturbed. But now I take a teaspoon and I begin to stir the water, and lo, immediately a cloud of milky, filthy material muddies the water and a stench rises from the glass. In the bottom of that quiet water was a layer of filth and dirt and germs, undetected until I stirred the water, and then it all came to light by the action of the teaspoon. Now the teaspoon did not pollute the water. The pollution was there all the time. The teaspoon merely stirred it up and revealed that it was there. Neither can the teaspoon purify that water. In order to do that I take the teaspoon OUT and lay it aside. Its work is done, and now I take the water and filter it, boil it, distill it, and then it is pure. Surely, because I lay the teaspoon aside because its work is done, you would not say the spoon was a failure because it could not make the water pure. The spoon was all right, but when its work of revealing the filth in the glass was done, it was laid aside. Nothing was wrong with the spoon.

The Spoon of the Law

Now study again the words of the text: "For when we were in the flesh, the MOTIONS (movements, agitations) of sins, which were BY THE LAW." When a thing moves it becomes visible, it becomes evident. While it is quiet it is undetected, but once it is put in motion, it becomes visible. And sin is set in motion by the law. The glass of water is your own heart. It looks very nice until it is stirred up. The spoon was the law which stirred up sin in the heart of man. Nothing was wrong with the law. It did not cause sin, neither can it purify the heart. It can only reveal the great need of the distillation of regeneration. No, the law, like the spoon, has done its perfect work, and it is not making the law void to say it is now set aside, since the need of purifying has been shown.

ANOTHER ILLUSTRATION

Let us illustrate in another way. When Mrs. De Haan and I were married, a bachelor uncle, to show his regard for our appetites, gave us as a wedding present a huge fruit bowl, probably eighteen inches across. It was so gigantic in size that we never could use it, and for years it was placed on the very top shelf of our pantry, and was only moved when housecleaning time came, and then was placed back on the shelf for another season. My boys had seen that bowl a hundred times and never had it aroused any curiosity in their minds. It was not especially attractive. But now suppose that on a certain day I take my son, and say, "Listen, son, do you see that big bowl up there in the cupboard?" and he answers, "Yes, daddy, what about it?" I say to him, "Don't you ever try to look in that bowl. If ever I find you trying to see what is in that bowl I am going to give you the soundest thrashing you have ever had." I repeat the commandment and repeat the penalty, and say, "Now, do you understand?" And he answers, "Yes, daddy." Now look! I have done something which has aroused in that boy's heart a desire for something he had never known before. Just as sure as he is a "chip off the old block" and the old block is a chip off the original block, Adam, he begins to wonder WHY he cannot look in that bowl. And just as sure as he sees me on my way, and mother has gone to do the shopping, he begins to fight an awful temptation he never had before. He wants to look in that fruit bowl, and if he weakens the least bit, he will set a chair on the table and a book on the chair and he is going to take one tiny peek to see WHY he cannot look in that bowl. THE MOTIONS OF SIN WHICH WERE BY THE LAW. I as his father did not do wrong by forbidding him to look. I as a father have a right to forbid him, to prove to him some things I want him to know. But while I was not the cause of his sin, I did stir up a desire in that child's heart which he never knew was there before. Do you see then WHY the law was given? It was to stir up sin and show us what a mess of corruption the human heart is, and how desperately we need the grace of God to save us.

> What shall we say then? Is the law sin? God forbid (Rom. 7:7a).

What the Law Could Not Do

The teaspoon could not make the water pure. My prohibition to my son could not make him better. My command, like the teaspoon, could only reveal the weakness of the flesh and the need of grace. The teaspoon could reveal the corruption, but it was powerless to correct it. So too the law revealed sin, but it was powerless to take it away. That is the next clear teaching of Paul.

> For what the law could NOT DO, in that it was weak through the flesh, God sending his own Son in the likeness of sinful flesh, and for sin, CONDEMNED SIN in the flesh: That the RIGHTEOUSNESS OF THE LAW might be

fulfilled in us, who walk not after the flesh, but after the Spirit (Rom. 8:3, 4).

WHAT THE LAW COULD NOT DO! There are some things the law CANNOT DO. There are some things the LAW was NEVER MEANT TO DO, and that is, to CREATE RIGHTEOUSNESS. On the contrary, it was given to REVEAL UNRIGHTEOUSNESS and the sinfulness of the flesh. That is why Jesus had to die on the Cross, because man could not be justified by the works of the law. Now there was nothing wrong with the law, but it was the weakness of the flesh, and the law condemned sin in the flesh that the RIGHTEOUSNESS of the law—NOT THE LAW—but the RIGHTEOUS-NESS of the law might be fulfilled in us.

Grace Alone

How sad indeed that after all the clear teaching of the Word there are still so few people who know the simplicity of grace and salvation through faith in the finished work of the Lord Jesus. One teaches that we are SAVED by keeping the law, another that we are KEPT by keeping the law, while still others say that the law brings us to Christ. Now some may object to that latter statement and refer me to the passage which is often quoted as saying that "the law was our schoolmaster to bring us to Christ." This passage is found in Galatians 3:24. But with your Bibles open before you, look at that 24th verse in Galatians 3:

> Wherefore the law was our schoolmaster (or pedagogue) to bring us unto Christ, that we might be justified by faith (Gal. 3:24).

Notice the words "our," "us," and "we." Wherever the pronouns "we," "us," and "our," occur, Paul is speaking of Israel. When the pronouns "ye" and "you" are used, it refers to the Gentiles. That is the key to the Book of Galatians. Now notice verse 24:

Wherefore the law WAS our schoolmaster (Gal. 3:24).

He says it WAS (past tense) OUR (that is, the Jews') schoolmaster. Nowhere do we read that the LAW IS a schoolmaster—IT WAS. But its work is done. Then the rest of the verse says TO BRING US to Christ. But the three words, "to bring us," are in italics, denoting that they are not in the original but were supplied by the translators. So leave out the italicized words from the verse and we read it this way as God gave it originally:

Wherefore the law WAS OUR schoolmaster UNTO CHRIST.

It was Israel's pedagogue until Christ should come, and then follows the next verse:

But after that faith is come, we are no longer under a schoolmaster.

For YE (Gentile Christians) are all the children of God BY FAITH in Christ Jesus (Gal. 3:25, 26).

His Righteousness

The law then cannot save. It cannot make us better. It can only condemn the sinner and show his great need of the grace of God. For what the law could not do, Jesus did, that—

The righteousness of the law might be fulfilled in us, who walk not after the flesh, but after the Spirit (Rom. 8:4).

The RIGHTEOUSNESS of the law is fulfilled in us. Not the LAW, but the RIGHTEOUSNESS of the law. That is, the righteousness of the Lord Jesus Christ is imputed to, and fulfilled in those who, looking away from the law, turn to Calvary for salvation. Jesus did two things. First, HE KEPT THE LAW PERFECTLY dur-

ing His thirty-three years on earth. Second, HE PAID
THE PENALTY of the law when He took its curse,
death, upon Himself. By His life He provided the righteousness of the law, and by His death He paid the penalty
of the law. And now the sinner turning to Christ receives
two things, both in Christ. First, he is freed from the
curse and the penalty of the law the moment he believes,
and God reckons the death of Christ as full payment for
the sinner's guilt and condemnation.

> ... He that heareth my word, and BELIEVETH on him
> that sent me, hath everlasting life, and shall not come into
> condemnation; but is passed from death unto life (John
> 5:24).

Then, secondly, God imputes to that forgiven sinner
the RIGHTEOUSNESS of Christ's sinless life, and by
that act the pardoned sinner becomes a justified saint.
That means that God now looks upon him IN CHRIST,
clothed in the perfect righteousness of His Son, Jesus.
In Christ he is as perfect as the Son of God Himself.
In Christ he is JUSTIFIED from all things from which
he could not be justified by the Law of Moses. In Christ
he is safe, for he is clothed in Christ's righteousness, and
God cannot ever turn that down.

Oh, friend, are you clothed in the righteousness of
Christ, or are you trying to save yourself by your own
works, either trying to keep the law TO BE SAVED, or
trying to keep the law to prevent losing salvation. Then
your case is hopeless. The Scripture says:

> For as many as are of the works of the law are under the
> curse: for it is written, Cursed is EVERY ONE that con-
> tinueth not in all things which are written in the book
> of the law to do them (Gal. 3:10).

Chapter Seventeen

FROM BONDAGE TO LIBERTY

THE churches of Galatia, founded during Paul's first missionary journey, had been thrown into confusion by the teachings of certain legalistic bigots who told these Gentile converts that they had to become Jewish proselytes by being circumcised and submitting themselves to the Law of Moses, with its rituals, ordinances and its curse. Failing to do so would forfeit their salvation. Paul's letter to the Galatians was written to counteract this error, and to prove that both Jew and Gentile are today saved by grace through faith without the works of the law, and are kept by grace, as well. We have pointed out in our past messages that the Law was:

1. Dispensational—John 1:17
2. National—Romans 2:14, 15
3. Experimental—Romans 3:19
4. Demonstrational—Romans 4:15
5. Revelational—Romans 7:5
6. Impossible—Romans 8:3

We now add a seventh reason for the giving of the law, and we shall call it

EDUCATIONAL

The law was given for a period of time as a rigid training to prepare us for the grace of God. And so Paul says that:

> ... the law was our schoolmaster to bring us unto (up
> to) Christ, that we might be justified by faith (Gal. 3:24).

The word "schoolmaster" may be translated "pedagogue" or child-trainer. Among the Greeks and Romans
certain persons, often specially trained servants, were
given custody over the children in the home, and were
responsible for their training in preparation for taking
their places of responsibility as mature sons in the home.
This training was often rigid and severe, so that when the
child reached maturity as an adult he would be fitted
to take his place, and honorably meet the claims and
responsibilities of sonship. When the child became an
adult, he was released from his "taskmaster," his training period ended, he takes his place as a son, and now
serves the father—not by restraint or threats of punishment and discipline, but voluntarily and willingly. The
period of the Law reaching from Moses to Christ, was
a time of education and training to prove that we could
not earn our salvation, but must receive it by grace. And
so Paul says that the "law was up to" or "until" Christ,
that we might be justified by faith.

> But after that faith is come, we are no longer under a
> schoolmaster (Gal. 3:25).

No language could be plainer. The law was our
schoolmaster "up to" Christ, but when He came, we were
no longer under the schoolmaster. We now have another
teacher, even the Spirit of Truth. Jesus said of Him:

> I have yet many things to say unto you, but ye cannot
> bear them now.
> Howbeit when he, the Spirit of truth, is come, he will
> guide you into all truth (John 16:12, 13).

The Holy Spirit came to reveal truth which the apostles
were not ready to receive before Pentecost. This was re-

served for the special revelation given to the apostles, Paul in particular. Before Christ came, revelation was in type and shadow. The Old Testament saints could not see what we see. The Old Testament saints since Moses were under the bondage of the law—the New Testament saint is in the liberty of the grace of God. In the Old Testament, the believer though an heir was an infant, while today we have received the standing as adult sons. This Paul asserts in Galatians 4,

> Now I say, that the heir, as long as he is a child, differeth nothing from a servant, though he be lord of all;
> But is under tutors and governors until the time appointed of the father.
> Even so we (Jews), when we were children (under the law), were in bondage under the elements of the world (Gal. 4:1-3).

The Old Testament saint was a babe, immature, not realizing the glory and fullness of his future inheritance. He was like a little child who, although heir to millions by virtue of relation to his father, is totally ignorant of the great wealth he is heir to, and would be made happier with a nickel than the promise of millions. A child cannot comprehend the meaning of a "million." It means nothing to him, but a nickel or a dime—he is perfectly satisfied with that. So the Old Testament saint lived in the shadows, saw things indistinctly and dimly. But today under grace the shadows are gone and we have the full revelation of our sonship.

The Difference?

Now what made the difference? It was the coming of Christ, and so Paul continues in Galatians 4:4,

> But when the fulness of time was come, God sent forth his Son, made of a woman, made under the law,

To redeem them that were under the law (as children),
that we might receive the adoption of sons (Gal. 4:4, 5).

The Cross stands between Law and Grace. Before
the Cross, there was no "putting away" of sin. God
pardoned the believer, suspended judgment, covered up
his sin, in anticipation of the coming of the Redeemer.
God pardoned the saints before Calvary upon the promise
of the coming of Christ. Before Calvary there was no
FULL forgiveness for the sinner, but after Calvary sin
is put away. Before Calvary, the sinner was pardoned;
after Calvary the sinner is justified by grace upon the
full payment of the penalty of the law by the death and
resurrection of Christ. Before Calvary no one could go
to Heaven, but was placed in sheol, till sin should be put
away (Psalm 16:9, 10). After Calvary, the believer at
death goes (not to sheol) but directly into the presence
of God in Heaven, absent from the body but present with
the Lord.

THE FULLNESS OF TIME

Jesus came in the fullness of time to redeem those
who were under the law. The expression, "fullness of
time," is explained in verse 2. It was the "time appointed
of the Father." Whereas Israel was compared to an irresponsible child, under the strict discipline of the law,
we today are adult sons and take our place fully in the
family of God. We are now "placed" as mature sons of
God. In this connection we call attention again to a very
important key to the understanding of Galatians. It is
in the use of the two pronouns, "we" and "us." Paul was
a Jew, writing to Gentiles. Wherever, therefore, the
pronoun "we" or "us" is used, it always refers to Israel,
but the "ye" and "you" always refer to the Gentiles.

Remember this, and it will make the study of Galatians much easier. As an example consider Galatians 3:23,

> But before faith came, we (Jews) were kept under the law . . .
>
> Wherefore the law was our (Jews') schoolmaster to bring us unto Christ, that we (Jews) might be justified by faith.
>
> But after that faith is come, we (Jews) are no longer under a schoolmaster.
>
> For ye (Gentiles) are all the children of God by faith in Christ Jesus.
>
> For as many of you (Gentiles) as have been baptized into Christ have put on Christ.
>
> And if ye (Gentiles) be Christ's, then are ye (Gentiles, also) Abraham's seed, and heirs according to the promise (Gal. 3:23-27, 29).

Apply this rule, remembering that when Paul says "we" he refers to Israel, and when he says "ye" it applies to the Gentiles. It will prevent you from mixing law and grace as these Galatians were doing.

BEFORE AND AFTER CALVARY

Before Christ came, Israel was under the tutorage of the law. This Paul asserts in Galatians 4:3,

> Even so we (Jews), when we were children, were in bondage under the elements of the world:
>
> But when the fulness of the time was come, God sent forth his Son, made of a woman, made under the law,
>
> To redeem them (the Jews) that were under the law, that we (Jews) might receive the adoption of sons (mature children).
>
> And because ye (Gentile believers) are sons, God hath sent forth the Spirit of his Son into your hearts, crying, Abba, Father.
>
> Wherefore thou art no more a servant, but a son; and if a son, then an heir of God through Christ (Gal. 4:3-7).

Those who are under the law are servants; those who are under grace are sons. A servant works for wages;

a son works through love and personal interest. There
is a great difference between working for a boss and for
a father. Under the law as boss, the service was by command and threat of penalty; under grace it is out of love
for our "Father."

A New Testament Title

Only under grace can we fully understand the meaning of "Our Father . . ." No saint in the Old Testament
fully realized the relationship of God as a Father, for
they were servants. Only after Pentecost was the meaning
of true sonship realized. The disciples asked Jesus to
teach them to pray, and He said, when ye pray say, "Our
Father which art in heaven." But the disciples never
used it, not even once until AFTER PENTECOST.
Paul used it for the first time in Romans 1:7 where he
calls God "our Father." The difference, therefore, of
being under law or under grace is the difference between
a slave and a son. A slave cannot call his master, "father";
it is reserved only for children. But Paul uses another
expression never used until after Calvary. It is ABBA,
Father. No one seems to know what the true meaning of
"abba" really is. It is not Hebrew nor Aramaic nor
Greek. It seems to be a term of intimacy, of affection and
endearment, indicating the closest possible relationship.
It is used only three times in Scripture, once in Mark
14:36, where Jesus in His agony in Gethsemane cries:

> Abba, Father, all things are possible unto thee; take away
> this cup from me (Mark 14:36).

The second time it is used in Romans 8:15, where
Paul says:

> For ye have not received the spirit of bondage again to
> fear (that is, the fear of the law); but ye have received the
> Spirit of adoption, whereby we cry, Abba, Father.

> The Spirit itself (himself) beareth witness with our spirit, that we are the children of God (Rom. 8:15, 16).

The third time the word "Abba" is used is in our passage in Galatians 4:6. It is then a term used only by the children of God who are under grace, being contrasted to the position of a servant under the law, and called the "spirit of bondage again to fear" (Rom. 8:15).

BACK UNDER THE LAW

What folly, therefore, to go back to the slavery of the law after being adopted as a son by grace! This was the thing which amazed and disturbed Paul so greatly, and he writes in astonishment:

> Howbeit then, when ye knew not God, ye did service unto them which by nature are no gods.
>
> But now, after that ye have known God, or rather are known of God, how turn ye again to the weak and beggarly elements, whereunto ye desire again to be in bondage? (Gal. 4:8, 9).

You who were delivered from your pagan religious rites, ceremonies and rituals and empty works into the grace and liberty of Christ, how can you turn back to put yourself under the laws, rituals, ceremonies and bondage of a fulfilled Judaism and legalism. "Ye observe days and months and times and years." What happened to you? says Paul.

> Where is then the (former) blessedness ye spake of? (Gal. 4:15).

Where is that first love and joy you had at the first, and your love for me so great you would have given me your eyes in exchange for my weak ones (Gal. 4:15)? How comes it that I am now become your enemy? What a tragedy that these people who had been won to Christ by Paul, should so soon turn upon him and lose their love for him. And that is the test of grace. Those who preach the law are always intolerant of the exponents of grace. The fruit of true grace is love and tender regard for those who disagree. How tenderly Paul pleads with these wayward Christians in an effort to correct their error which was destroying their joy and victory.

Application to Us

Apply this test to yourself. Does the thing you believe make you kind and loving and zealous to win men and women to Christ? Or does it make you critical, condemnatory, bigoted and intolerant? Do you seek to win men and women to Christ, or are you seeking to proselyte believers to your sectarian, legalistic views? The false teachers in Paul's day were not out winning souls for Christ, but rather seeking to unsettle believers by their legalistic doctrine of works. Oh, that we might be more interested in preaching the grace of God to lost sinners, than going about arguing doctrines, promoting a sect or organization, or denomination. God help us to grow in grace, and in the knowledge of our Lord Jesus Christ.

Chapter Eighteen

THE TALE OF TWO CITIES

Tell me, ye that desire to be under the law, do ye not hear the law? (Gal. 4:21).

THE question the Apostle Paul seeks to answer in Galatians was a question of law OR grace. It was not law AND grace, but law OR grace. It cannot be both. It is either one or the other. To say that we are saved by grace, and then kept by our works is to negate grace entirely, for then our final salvation depends upon our behavior and works instead of the grace of God. The desire to be kept by the works of the law is the result of a total misunderstanding of what the law really is and does. Once we understand the true purpose of the law, we would never want to be placed under it again. And so Paul asks the question, "Tell me, ye that desire to be under the law, don't you understand what the law does?" And then follows an allegory, and a figurative contrast between law and grace. Here is Paul's argument:

For it is written, that Abraham had two sons, the one by a bondmaid, the other by a freewoman.

But he who was of the bondwoman was born after the flesh; but he of the freewoman was by promise.

Which things are an allegory: for these are the two covenants; the one from the mount Sinai, which gendereth to bondage, which is Agar.

For this Agar is mount Sinai in Arabia, and answereth

to Jerusalem which now is, and is in bondage with her
children.

But Jerusalem which is above is free, which is the mother
of us all (Gal. 4:22-26).

Paul in his eagerness to show the striking difference
between law and grace, and that they cannot be mixed,
refers the Galatian Christians to an incident in history—
or rather, a number of incidents from Israel's history.
First, he reminds them that Abraham had two wives,
a bondmaiden and his permanent wife, Sarah. He con-
trasts Hagar, the Egyptian slave woman, with Sarah, the
wife of promise, and likens Hagar to the law, and Sarah
to the grace of God. Next, he introduces two sons,
Ishmael, son of Hagar, born after the flesh by the will
of man, and Isaac, supernaturally born by promise. Now,
says Paul, these two women, Hagar and Sarah, and these
two sons, Ishmael and Isaac, are an allegory; that is, they
have a spiritual application. They are symbolic of law
and grace—the allegory Paul uses to illustrate his teaching
of grace. It is taking a historical incident as a symbol,
figure or illustration of some spiritual truth. The story
of Abraham and Hagar and the birth of Ishmael after
the flesh is not a mere incident in the history of Abraham,
but is recorded to teach a far deeper, more profound
lesson. It is this—Ishmael was born of the will of the
flesh, and revealed Abraham's terrible failure and weakness in trying to help God in fulfilling the promise of
a son. Abraham had given up his hope that Sarah would
give birth to a seed. But God had promised to Abraham
a seed, and so Abraham seeks to help God in keeping His
promise by raising up a seed by Hagar the bondwoman—
symbol of bondage, failure and doubt. This act of Abraham, says Paul, is illustrative of man's attempt to please
God by the works of the law. Hagar corresponds to the

law. Ishmael is representative of the works of the flesh, and gendereth bondage.

EXPANDS THE ALLEGORY

Paul then explains the allegory. Ishmael symbolizes the covenant of the law given on Sinai. Notice again the clear teaching:

> Which things (the birth of Ishmael and Isaac) are an allegory: for these are the two covenants; the one from the mount Sinai, which gendereth to bondage, which is Agar.
> For this Agar (Hagar, mother of Ishmael) is mount Sinai in Arabia, and answereth to Jerusalem which now is, and is in bondage with her children (Gal. 4:24, 25).

In addition to two women, Hagar and Sarah, and two sons, Ishmael and Isaac, Paul now introduces two covenants—the covenant of the law on Mount Sinai, and the covenant of grace ratified on Mount Calvary. Then he adds two cities—the Jerusalem of Paul's day, and the future New Jerusalem, the eternal abode of the redeemed and the free. So notice carefully the allegory. We have:

1. Two women—Hagar and Sarah
2. Two sons—Ishmael and Isaac
3. Two covenants—law and grace
4. Two mountains—Sinai and Calvary
5. Two cities—earthly Jerusalem
   and heavenly Jerusalem

Now all this detail is to show the difference between law and grace. Hagar, Ishmael, Mount Sinai and historic Jerusalem are pictures of the law. Hagar was a slave, and the law enslaves. How can anyone cling to the law for help in the face of Paul's words in verse 24 where he says that the covenant of the law is:

> . . . from the mount Sinai, which gendereth to bondage (Gal. 4:24).

To further nail it down Paul continues and says that the law, given on Mount Sinai could not set anyone free, but brings only bondage. Look at Israel's city of Jerusalem. What is her condition? Once she was the proud capital of Palestine, the seat of the mighty King David, the envy of the world in the days of Solomon! Look at her now, in bondage to a foreign Gentile power, the nation stripped of her freedom, and Jerusalem the seat of a pagan Roman governor. And why? Because Israel tried to be kept by the law, and rejected God's grace. Listen to Paul again:

> ... this Agar is mount Sinai ... and answereth to Jerusalem which now is, AND IS IN BONDAGE WITH HER CHILDREN (Gal. 4:25).

Hagar—Ishmael—Sinai—the law—earthly Jerusalem, are all pictures of the law. It could not make Hagar free or make Ishmael the heir of promise. Sinai had no message of hope for Israel. God's covenant of works offered no salvation to Israel, but only condemnation, bondage and judgment.

We would repeat with Paul the verse with which this allegory is introduced: "Tell me, ye that desire to be under the law, will you listen for just a moment until I tell you what the law really does?"

The New Jerusalem

Having shown that the law can only gender bondage, Paul now shows the glory of grace. He says:

> But Jerusalem which is above is FREE, which is the mother of us all (Gal. 4:26).

The law genders fear; grace brings peace and assurance. In Hebrews 12 we have possibly the sharpest contrast between law and grace in the Scriptures. Here the apostle says to those who are saved by grace:

For ye are not come unto the mount that might be touched, and that burned with fire, nor unto blackness, and darkness, and tempest,

And the sound of a trumpet, and the voice of words; which voice they that heard intreated that the word should not be spoken to them any more:

(For they could not endure that which was commanded, And if so much as a beast touch the mountain, it shall be stoned, or thrust through with a dart:

And so terrible was the sight, that Moses said, I exceedingly fear and quake:)

But ye are come unto mount Sion, and unto the city of the living God, the heavenly Jerusalem, and to an innumerable company of angels.

To the general assembly and church of the firstborn, which are written in heaven, and to God the Judge of all, and to the spirits of just men made perfect,

And to Jesus the mediator of the new covenant, and to the blood of sprinkling, that speaketh better things than that of Abel (Heb. 12:18-24).

Read carefully the account of the giving of the law in Exodus 19:9-13 and Exodus 20, beginning at verse 18.

Cast out the Bondwoman

Paul concludes his allegory in a most positive way:

... Rejoice, thou barren that bearest not; break forth and cry, thou that travailest not: for the desolate hath many more children than she which hath an husband (Gal. 4:27).

Hagar was first to bear—Ishmael was the firstborn in Abraham's tent. So too the law was given first, before grace and truth were revealed by Jesus Christ. "For the law was given by Moses, but grace and truth came by Jesus Christ" (John 1:17). As the firstborn Ishmael was set aside, and the younger son, Isaac, was heir of promise, so the law which was first, could not save, and must be abandoned as a means of salvation and justification, and we must be saved by grace alone. The first becomes last, and the last becomes first. This is the force of the allegory of the barren wife (Sarah) becoming fruitful, while the bondwoman (Hagar) is set aside. Grace supersedes the law. Notice the conclusion:

> Now we, brethren, as Isaac was, are the children of promise.
> But as then he that was born after the flesh persecuted him that was born after the Spirit, even so it is now.
> Nevertheless what saith the scripture? Cast out the bondwoman and her son: for the son of the bondwoman shall not be heir with the son of the freewoman.
> So then, brethren, we are not children of the bondwoman, but of the free (Gal. 4:28-31).

Things have not changed. The descendants of the legalists of Paul's day are with us today to persecute and oppose our message of grace. The most violent and vicious opposition we receive in our ministry is from those who would place us back under the law, and to proselyte the children of grace by seeking to turn them again to the weak and beggarly elements, to observe days and months and times and years. To all such we answer in the words of Paul in Colossians 2:

> Let no man therefore judge you in meat, or in drink, or in respect of an holyday, or of the new moon, or of the sabbath days:
> Which are a shadow of things to come; but the body is of Christ (Col. 2:16, 17).

The true believer does not serve the Lord because HE MUST or be lost. He does not serve God out of fear, but out of a heart of gratitude and thankfulness for having been delivered from the curse of the law. Any other service is bondage instead of liberty. In our next message, therefore, we shall begin with Galatians 5:1,

Stand fast therefore in the liberty wherewith Christ hath made us free, and be not entangled again with the yoke of bondage (Gal. 5:1).

We conclude, therefore, with Paul that "no man is justified by the law in the sight of God" (Gal. 3:11).

Failure to save is not the fault of the law. The inability of the law to justify a sinner is not a sign of the law's failure or weakness. The law cannot, nor is it expected to save a sinner. That was not the purpose of the law. God gave the law to PROVE that man could not be saved by LAW WORKS, that it might convince mankind of the need of the grace of God, and get them ready to accept the grace of God in Christ Jesus. The law is perfect; that is why imperfect men cannot keep it. The law is holy; that is why sinners are condemned by it. The law is just, and therefore cannot show mercy to the guilty, for that would be in violation of its justness and justice. The perfect law can only show the nature of sin. The law condemns and says, "Cursed is every one that continueth not in all things which are written in the book of the law to do them" (Gal. 3:10).

1. The law prohibits—Grace invites and gives.
2. The law condemns the sinner—Grace redeems the sinner.
3. The law says DO—Grace says IT IS DONE.
4. The law says, Continue to be holy—Grace says, It is finished.
5. The law curses—Grace blesses.
6. The law slays the sinner—Grace makes the sinner alive.
7. The law shuts every mouth before God—Grace opens the mouth to praise God.

8. The law condemns the best man—Grace saves the worst man.

9. The law says, pay what you owe—Grace says, I freely forgive you all.

10. The law says "the wages of sin is death"—Grace says, "the gift of God is eternal life."

11. The law says, "the soul that sinneth it shall die"—Grace says, Believe and live.

12. The law reveals sin—Grace atones for sin.

13. By the law is the knowledge of sin—By grace is redemption from sin.

14. The law was given by Moses—Grace and truth came by Jesus Christ.

15. The law demands obedience—Grace bestows and gives power to obey.

16. The law was written on stone—Grace is written on the tables of the heart.

17. The law was done away in Christ—Grace abides forever.

18. The law puts us under bondage—Grace sets us in the liberty of the sons of God.

And so we might go on to show how the Bible definitely distinguishes between the two. We serve God now, because we are under grace, and Paul says in Romans 21:1,

> I beseech you therefore, brethren, by the mercies of God, that ye present your bodies a living sacrifice, holy, acceptable unto God, which is your reasonable service (Rom. 12:1).

Chapter Nineteen

THE LABOR OF LOVE

> Stand fast therefore in the liberty wherewith Christ hath
> made us free, and be not entangled again with the yoke
> of bondage (Gal. 5:1).

THE fifth chapter of Galatians begins the application
of the doctrinal truths set forth in the first four chapters.
At great length Paul had tried to show these Galatians
the folly of being swayed by certain false teachers, who
asserted that while we are saved by grace, we are still
obligated to keep the law of God perfectly or again lose
our salvation. They were told they must keep the ordinances, become circumcised, observe legal restrictions,
keep the sabbath days, and place themselves under the
law of commandments given to Israel. With unassailable
logic Paul had asserted that the believer is saved by grace,
justified by grace, kept by grace, and in the end will be
saved by grace. The believer is free from the law (Rom.
8:2), dead to the law (Gal. 2:19), delivered from the law
(Rom. 7:6), for—

> ... Christ is the end of the law for righteousness to
> every one that believeth (Rom. 10:4).

He concludes his argument with the verses:

> ... Cast out the bondwoman and her son ...
> So then, brethren, we are not children of the bondwoman
> (the law), but of the FREE (grace) (Gal. 4:30, 31).

Free from the Law

Notice the last word of the doctrinal section of Galatians, FREE! FREE! The believer is free, set at liberty, delivered. Salvation by grace means deliverance and freedom. There is no bondage for those who are in Christ. Now as we shall see, liberty does not mean license to sin; freedom does not mean we are not accountable for our conduct. This Paul makes clear in Galatians 5:13. We are free indeed—not free to sin—but free to serve the Lord without fear and compulsion. This we have seen in Galatians 2:19, where we are said to be DEAD to the law, but ALIVE unto God. Someone asked a certain preacher of grace, "Do you mean to say that if I am saved by grace, I can do as I want to?" The servant of God replied, "Yes, if you are saved you can do as you want to, but remember, if you are saved, really saved, God gave you a different 'want to'—you WANT TO serve God."

Stand Fast

Now notice how the next chapter begins after closing chapter 4 with the word, FREE.

> Stand fast therefore in the liberty (freedom) wherewith Christ hath made us free, and be not entangled again with the yoke of bondage (Gal. 5:1).

The admonition was sorely needed, for the temptation to go back under the law in order to avoid persecution and loss of friends was very great. They would be accused of being anti-nomian and lawless, and guilty of making the grace of God an occasion for license and sin. But in spite of all this Paul says, "Stand fast!" To go back is to take again the yoke of bondage from which Christ had set them free. Even the apostles in Jerusalem admitted that the law was a yoke which neither they nor their fathers were able to bear (Acts 15:10).

DEBTOR TO THE WHOLE LAW

We go on now into the succeeding verses for Paul's argument to stand fast in the liberty and freedom of grace:

> Behold, I Paul say unto you, that if ye be circumcised, Christ shall profit you nothing.
>
> For I testify again to every man that is circumcised, that he is a debtor to do the whole law.
>
> Christ is become of no effect unto you, whosoever of you are justified by the law; ye are fallen from grace.
>
> For we through the Spirit wait for the hope of righteousness by faith.
>
> For in Jesus Christ neither circumcision availeth any thing, nor uncircumcision; but faith which worketh by love (Gal. 5:2-6).

The legalistic teachers had insisted that the Gentiles, to be saved must become Jews and submit to the rite of circumcision. This Paul vigorously opposes and says, "If you submit to circumcision you become debtor to the whole law and are under its curse and condemnation. Christ then can profit you nothing." It is not law AND grace—but law OR grace. It must be all grace, or it is not grace at all. To look to the law for justification is to miss the grace of God. This is the force of verse 4:

> Christ is become of no effect unto you, whosoever of you are justified (seek to be justified) by the law; ye are fallen from grace (Gal. 5:4).

The word "fallen" in this verse is "ekpipto" and means literally "to have been driven out of one's course," as of sailors who have been driven out of their normal lane. It is the same word used in Acts 27, in the account of the shipwreck. Luke says in Acts 27:17 that the sailors feared—

> ... lest they should FALL into the quicksands, strake sail (lowered the sails) (Acts 27:17).

In verse 29 of Acts 27 we read:

> Then fearing lest we should have FALLEN upon rocks, they cast four anchors out of the stern, and wished for the day (Acts 27:29).

From this we may see the meaning of the expression, "fallen from grace." You who think you can be saved or kept by the law—you have been driven out of course, and missed the grace of God. Paul was greatly distressed at their conduct. Had he been mistaken when he believed they were truly converted? He says in Galatians 4:11,

> I am afraid of you, lest I have bestowed upon you labour in vain (Gal. 4:11).

I am in doubt about you, as a result of your following these false teachers of the law. Paul would permit no tampering with the grace of God. Rather, therefore, than relying upon the works of the law, Paul says:

> For we through the Spirit wait for the hope of righteousness BY FAITH.
> For in Jesus Christ neither circumcision availeth any thing, nor uncircumcision; but FAITH WHICH WORK-ETH BY LOVE (Gal. 5:5, 6).

Shall We Sin?

In declaring that salvation is liberty and freedom from the law, an objection was anticipated. The question would be raised: If salvation is all of grace without works, then is there no place for works in the Christian life at all? To be sure there is, as the fruit of salvation. Works are not the ROOT or basis of salvation, but they are the inevitable, indispensable FRUIT. If a person professing to be saved by grace continues in sin, or makes grace an occasion for loose living and careless conduct, we have a right to question that one's sincerity and reality. As surely as we are saved by grace, so surely it must be manifested by our works. How wonderfully it is expressed by Paul in the words,

FAITH WHICH WORKETH BY LOVE.

Saving faith is a WORKING faith. If it doesn't work, it is not saving faith. Then Paul adds, "BY LOVE." Faith which worketh, by love—not by law. A servant works by laws and rules and regulations. But love knows nothing about rules and restrictions, for "love is the fulfilling of the law." Yes, love is the fulfilling of the law, but it is also much more, for it goes way beyond the demands of the law. If a man keeps the law of the land, he fulfills his duty, and he needs to do no more. But if he loves his country, he will do more than just abide by its laws—he will seek to promote its welfare, support worthy civic projects, exercise his liberty to vote and support the government in every way. He will take part in social, civic and benevolent projects. The law does not compel him to do these things. It merely demands obedience only to the laws on the books. But love goes way beyond the demands of the law. Love does not ask, how little can I do and still get by? but how much more can I do?

To the charge that freedom from the law genders carelessness, looseness of living and license, we can only answer that such a charge is due to ignorance of the power of grace. The grace of God becomes our teacher through the Holy Spirit within us. Once we truly understand grace and that we are delivered from the law, LOVE takes over and goes way beyond the demands of the law. It is faith which worketh by LOVE.

> For all the law is fulfilled in one word, even in this; Thou shalt love thy neighbour as thyself (Gal. 5:14).

SERVANT OR LOVER?

While I was still practicing medicine, we had servants in our home, to do some of the work. We had a maid for the housework, and I had a chauffeur to drive the car for me. They were servants. They worked for wages. Their duties were clearly defined and they knew just exactly how much was expected of them. They were to work certain hours, do certain duties, and for this they were to receive stipulated wages. The rules and regulations were plain. For instance, the maid must be there at 8:00 a.m. and with an hour for lunch she worked until 5:00 p.m. She received her two meals a day, was allowed to have Wednesday afternoon off. She was allowed a certain amount of time for sick leave and other fringe benefits. As long as she met her obligations she received so much per week. We could expect no more from her. She had fulfilled her legal obligations and we had no further claim on her.

COMES THE WIFE

Now compare such an arrangement with the service of another person in our home—my wife. She is not a servant. She does not work for wages. We have no agreement concerning hours or pay. Her duties are not outlined and spelled out for her. She knows nothing about a time clock. Eight o'clock starting time and five o'clock quitting time mean nothing to her. She never thinks about wages, never goes on strike, but gives her unceasing, willing service to the home and family twenty-four hours a day and fifty-two weeks in the year. She is under no law or rules or stipulations, nor is there any need for them. I have never told her to do a thing, for she knows what her family needs, and fulfills it before anyone needs to ask. No need to tell her to dress the children, feed the baby, humor the "old man," wash the dishes and make the beds. There is no grumbling or complaining. She gets weary and tired, but love keeps her going. If the servant is told to put in a little over-time, there is grumbling and dragging of feet—she is a servant. But Mrs. De Haan doesn't know what the term "overtime" means. She doesn't ask for double-time pay for working on Saturday or Sunday. And why not? You know the answer. It is LOVE which motivates her service. She delights to give herself to her family because she loves them. And because of her unstinting, loving devotion, there is no place for laws, rules, regulations or commandments in our home. It is a labor of love. The service of love goes way beyond the demands of the law.

So it is also in the family of God. The true believer is free from the law of commandments and is under the perfect law of liberty and of love. Can you imagine a wife and mother in a family which she devotedly loves, and having the liberty to do as she pleases and serve as she wishes, demanding or desiring to be put on a servant's basis with sharply defined rules, stipulated hours of service, and prearranged wages? Suppose I say to my wife, "You are working too hard. From now on you work only from 8 to 5, and then you are free the rest of the time— and I'll pay you $100.00 a week." What do you suppose she would say? "Keep your $100.00 and your shorter

hours. I want to be with my family and serve them ALL
THE TIME." But I want her to work from 8 to 5. To
this she answers, "I already work from 8 to 5, and in
addition I want to serve from 5 to 8, not for wages but
for love." This is "faith which worketh by love." What
shall we say then of Christians saved by grace who want
to go back under the law? You ask me, "Do not Christians
who are under grace have to keep the law?" No, there is
no compulsion, but the truly born-again believer desires
to keep the law, not because he MUST, but because he
WANTS TO, and goes far beyond the demands of the
law itself. Yet the Galatian legalists would convince us
to go back under bondage, and rob us of the joy of serving
out of a heart of love. If we love as we ought to love,
we need no one to tell us what to do—for the grace of
God will teach us through His Word and His Spirit.
We will then cease judging another's liberty in Christ.

Oh, for the grace to put into practice this principle of
Paul and cease forever this judging and condemning of
other believers because they do not agree with us in
every minor detail. There are those who condemn us
and tell us that we are forever destined to Hell if we do
not observe one certain day or follow some certain cus-
tom or ritual. Well, this passage should settle that question. It is not a matter of the day at all. It is a matter of
grace and of graciousness. The question is simply this,
"Are you under the law or under grace?" If you are
under the law, then by all means keep the commandments including every one of them; but remember, keep
them perfectly, for the Bible tells us that "he that offends
in one point is guilty of all." The language of the law is
very clear:

Cursed is every one that continueth not in all things

which are written in the book of the law to do them (Gal. 3:10).

That is the language of the law; but if you are under grace, and the law was fulfilled in Christ, then everything was fulfilled. We rejoice in the liberty which we have, and as an expression of our gratitude to Him, we serve Him with the fullness of our hearts, and with all our devotion, not for wages, but out of love.

Chapter Twenty

THE FRUIT OF THE SPIRIT

THE believer is delivered from the curse of the law (Gal. 3:13). He is placed in the freedom and liberty of grace, and now serves the Lord, not out of compulsion or threat of punishment, but out of a heart of love and gratitude for so great a salvation. It is therefore a contradiction for a person saved by grace to serve the Lord because the law demands it, rather than because love produces it. This liberty in grace also gives divine discernment as to what is required. There is, however, a danger, because the flesh is still with us, that we shall have a tendency to go back to the works of the flesh and the law. This was true in the case of the Galatians. Paul is surprised that they would be led astray by the legalistic teachers with the Old Testament ordinances, laws, sabbath days and commandments. He exhorts them:

> Stand fast therefore in the liberty wherewith Christ hath made us free, and be not entangled again with the yoke of bondage (Gal. 5:1).

In verse 7 he asks a question:

> Ye did run well; who did hinder you that ye should not obey the truth? (Gal. 5:7).

Who are these pious but false teachers who say you are saved by grace, and then kept by observing the law? Certainly they are not sent from God; that, says Paul, you may be sure of. With all their fair speeches and prat-

162

ing about the Gospel, it is not the message of grace. Notice Paul's indictment:

> This persuasion cometh not of him that calleth you (Gal. 5:8).

That teaching of the works of the law—mixing law and grace—is certainly not of the Lord, says Paul; for to add even the tiniest bit of works to grace spoils it all. If the works of the law have anything at all to do with salvation, then one must keep the whole law perfectly and uninterruptedly. The least bit of works, however, spoils it all, and so he continues:

> A little leaven leaveneth the whole lump (Gal. 5:9).

Leaven always refers to evil, evil in morals or evil in doctrine. In this case it is evil doctrine, the addition of works to grace. So serious did Paul consider this error that he uses the severest language in warning against it:

> I have confidence in you through the Lord, that ye will be none otherwise minded: but he that troubleth you shall bear his judgment, whosoever he be....
> I would they were even cut off which trouble you (Gal. 5:10, 12).

This indeed is strong language by the apostle. The verse may be translated, "I would they would even cut themselves off which trouble you."

Why don't they go all the way with their false teaching, instead of just harping on the rite of circumcision? Why don't they go all the way, and tell you you must put yourself under all the legal restrictions of sacrifices, offerings, rituals, dietary rules, sabbath days, and holydays? Their emphasis on the one issue—circumcision—is only a front, and when they have you to do this, they will then begin to feed you all their other errors, which they now keep in the background.

OFFENSE OF THE CROSS

That this is the meaning of the verse is clear from that
which Paul says in the preceding verse:

> And I, brethren, if I yet preach circumcision, why do I
> yet suffer persecution? then is the offence of the cross ceased
> (Gal. 5:11).

I could avoid all my persecution if I would only compromise a little bit and agree that salvation is by grace
PLUS circumcision—the law. But there is much more
involved for if I preach circumcision, I must preach the
entire law, the Ten Commandments and all the civil
and ceremonial laws as well. To separate between the
law of the Ten Commandments as the law of God, and
the ceremonial laws as the laws of Moses is gross de-
ception. And so, says Paul, "If I preach circumcision,
I must also preach all the rest of the law." Don't be
fooled, for there is far more involved than the mere rite
of circumcision. To say we are under part of the law,
or one commandment, may sound appealing, but it in-
volves the whole law. To say we must keep the legal
sabbath, for instance, is to place ourselves under the whole
law of commandments, rituals, and ordinances, dietary
rules and holy days. No! it is either ALL GRACE or
ALL LAW. It cannot be both. And if we are under
the law, we are under the curse. If we are under grace,
we are free from the law.

SHALL WE SIN?

Now a serious question arises. While we teach that
a believer should serve God perfectly out of a heart of
love and gratitude, and seek to keep God's law, and even
go beyond the demands of the law, it is an indisputable
fact that many Christians are not living holy lives, but
of all of us it may be said that we too often fall short of

God's perfect will. All of us are prone to fall. There is not a person who at the end of any one day can honestly say, "This day I have lived a perfect, holy life in thought, word, and deed. I have met every requirement of God's holy law. I have not wasted one second, I have not neglected one single duty. I have been my best in every act, I have left nothing undone I should have done, and have done all that was required of me." Every one who knows his own heart will confess that in his holiest endeavors he still comes short. For this, forgiveness is provided (I John 1:9). For this, strength is promised. In verse 14 Paul says:

> For all the law is fulfilled in one word, even this: Thou shalt love thy neighbour as thyself (Gal. 5:14).

But who can say that he has always done this? Instead, the next verse is too tragically, and often, true:

> But if ye bite and devour one another, take heed that ye be not consumed one of another (Gal. 5:15).

What then shall we do? Here is the answer (verse 16):

> This I say then, WALK in the Spirit, and ye shall not fulfil the lust of the flesh.
> For the flesh lusteth against the Spirit, and the Spirit against the flesh: and these are contrary the one to the other: so that ye cannot do the things that ye would.
> But if ye be led of the Spirit, ye are not under the law (Gal. 5:16-18).

Every believer still has within him the old nature—the flesh; it is not eradicated, but is to be made subject to, conquered by, the new nature. The terrible mistake made by so many misinformed Christians is trying to gain the victory by their own efforts, by the works of the law, instead of a complete yielding and surrender to the Spirit of God. Paul's advice is:

... Walk in the Spirit, and ye shall not fulfil the lust of the flesh (Gal. 5:16).

Our hope of victory lies not in the law, or our good resolutions and intentions, but in complete submission and yielding to the Spirit's word of grace. How clearly it is stated in Titus 2:11, 12,

> For the grace of God that bringeth salvation hath appeared to all men,
> Teaching us that, denying ungodliness and worldly lusts, we should live soberly, righteously, and godly, in this present world (Titus 2:11, 12).

And Paul states it again as follows:

> But if ye be led of the Spirit, ye are not under the law (Gal. 5:18).

An Illustration

Now follows an illustration and a striking contrast between the flesh and Spirit. Galatians 5:19 begins with:

> Now the works of the flesh are.... (Gal. 5:19).

But verse 22 begins with:

> But the fruit of the Spirit is.... (Gal. 5:22a).

Notice just two words, WORKS and FRUIT. Works of the flesh—Fruit of the Spirit. Works speak of effort, mechanics, toil and labor. Works result in weariness, faintness, and often frustration. It is accompanied by much fleshly effort, and much display and noise of hammer and saw. But FRUIT! How different! It does not involve work, but is the result of just RECEIVING, YIELDING, ACCEPTING. It means having no confidence in the flesh, but an honest confession of our weakness, an earnest plea for forgiveness, and a surrender to the will of God.

Paul gives a catalogue of the works of the flesh in verses 19 to 21:

> Now the works of the flesh are manifest, which are these; Adultery, fornication, uncleanness, lasciviousness,
> Idolatry, witchcraft, hatred, variance, emulations, wrath, strife, seditions, heresies,
> Envyings, murders, drunkenness, revellings, and such like: of the which I tell you before, as I have also told you in time past, that they which do such things shall not inherit the kingdom of God (Gal. 5:19-21).

These are the works of the old nature and must be overcome by walking in the Spirit (vs. 16), being led of the Spirit (vs. 18), and living in the Spirit (vs. 25). As we yield all to God, there follows the FRUIT of the Spirit:

> But the fruit of the Spirit is love, joy, peace, longsuffering, gentleness, goodness, faith,
> Meekness, temperance: against such there is no law (Gal. 5:22, 23).

These are not FRUITS but FRUIT. The "works" of the flesh are plural and Paul enumerates seventeen of them in detail. But the "fruit" of the Spirit is singular and consists of three groups of virtues:

1. Personal fruit—love, joy, peace. These have to do with our own subjective personal life.

2. Outreaching fruit to others—longsuffering, gentleness, goodness. This is our attitude in grace toward others.

3. Up-reaching fruit—toward God. They are faith, meekness, temperance. Nine parts of one fruit, all supplied by the Spirit. It covers our complete responsibility toward God, our fellow man, and others. It covers the whole ground of the law:

1. Duty toward God.

2. Duty toward others.
3. Duty toward self.

THE LAW OF LIBERTY

The question therefore is not, does the law forbid this or that? but how will my action affect the glory of God, my testimony before men, and my personal sanctification? When the flesh comes with its temptation, I need not run to the Ten Commandments to see if it forbids it. There are many things which may be wrong, yet are not specifically mentioned in the law. The question is rather: Is this honoring to God? Does it help my fellow man? Does it produce in me love, joy, and peace? On every doubtful matter, ask these questions: Will it glorify God? Will it help or hinder others? Will it promote my spirituality? If in doubt, DON'T DO IT.

May the Holy Spirit have His perfect way in our lives, and teach us that "denying ungodliness and worldly lusts, we should live soberly, righteously, and godly, in this present world" (Titus 2:12).

And why? Because we don't want to go to Hell? Definitely not! but instead, because we have been saved from Hell and damnation through Him,

> Who gave himself for us, that he might redeem us from all iniquity, and purify unto himself a peculiar people, zealous of good works (Titus 2:14).

Chapter Twenty-one

THE SIN OF JUDGING OTHERS

> Brethren, if a man be overtaken in a fault, ye which
> are spiritual, restore such an one in the spirit of meekness;
> considering thyself, lest thou also be tempted (Gal. 6:1).

IN the previous chapter (Gal. 5) Paul had given a general
view of the practical application of the doctrine of the
grace of God. He pointed out the evidences and proof
of our justification by faith, without the works of the
law. The difference between a legalist and a true believer
is evidenced by the rule with which a fellow man is
judged. The legalist measures a man by the law and finds
him to come short, and so resorts to criticism and condemnation. The believer who knows the grace of God,
however, is gracious, tolerant, merciful, longsuffering and
kind, and forgiving. The most caustic and condemnatory
letters we receive (and we receive plenty of them) are
from those ungracious people who object to our preaching of salvation by grace alone, and complete deliverance
from the law. Some people judge their fellow men by
the way they conduct their services, by the vestments
they wear, by the particular day they observe as the
Sabbath or the Lord's Day. I know people who base
their entire estimate of another's salvation on how the
Lord's Day or the so-called Sabbath is spent, while they
forget that the worst way to spend the Sabbath or Lord's
Day is in finding fault, criticizing and condemning those

who do not see eye to eye with them in their legalistic, hairsplitting traditions of men.

Love Not Criticism

This evil Paul was dead set against. Hence he closes chapter 5 with the admonition:

> Let us not be desirous of vain glory, provoking one another, envying one another (Gal. 5:26).

Paul's aim for the believer was perfection, absolute sinless perfection, but he realized that complete and perfect sanctification would not be realized until we reach the end of the road. Paul did not teach eradication of the old man of the flesh, but he exhorted them to victory of the new man over the old. It was Paul who wrote:

> For I know that in me (that is, in my flesh,) dwelleth no good thing (Rom. 7:18).

The apostle knew the subtlety and weakness of the old nature and asserted that he had no confidence in the flesh (Phil. 3:3).

When a sinner is converted, nothing happens to the old, sinful nature. It is so hopelessly, incorrigibly corrupt that God does not even attempt to improve it, convert it, change it, or make it better. Instead, He makes a new creature, the spiritual man, and places it in the believer ALONGSIDE the old man. The new birth is not a re-birth, but a NEW BIRTH from above. That which is born of the flesh remains flesh, and that which is born of the Spirit remains Spirit. This is where the struggle comes, and as Paul says:

> ... the flesh lusteth against the Spirit, and the Spirit against the flesh: and these are contrary the one to the other: so that ye cannot do the things that ye would (Gal. 5:17).

Our only hope is outside ourselves for victory. If we were to be saved by our sinless perfection, all would be lost. It must still be the grace of God which causes us to claim the victory THROUGH OUR LORD JESUS CHRIST.

Hence we have all the admonitions to go on, to grow in grace, to walk in the Spirit, to yield our members, to present our bodies, to press on toward the goal for the prize. If the believer were as perfect in his state and walk, as in his standing and position in Christ, there would be no need of admonition to "present our bodies a living sacrifice" (Rom. 12:1) or "walk in the Spirit." Why then the warning against Christian cannibalism in Galatians 5:15,

> But if ye bite and devour one another, take heed that ye be not consumed one of another (Gal. 5:15).

Christian cannibalism! What an indictment! And the remedy for our unkind conduct toward others is a better understanding of the grace of God. If we but remembered that Christ came to save us at infinite cost, when we were vile, wretched, miserable, filthy sinners on the way to Hell, without one single claim to God's mercy— I say, if we but remembered that, we would be more kind, considerate, sympathetic, forgiving, tenderhearted, and patient with other fellow believers.

WEAKER BRETHREN

But because we too often forget the pit from which we have been digged, we need the reminder of what we once were and the danger of what we may become. Paul therefore touches upon this thing as we begin Galatians 6:

> Brethren, if a man be overtaken in a fault, ye which are spiritual, restore such an one in the spirit of meekness; considering thyself, lest thou also be tempted (Gal. 6:1).

Notice in this verse, he is speaking to the "brethren," believers, about their treatment of a fallen brother. They are not to judge, censure and condemn, but restore such an one. The backslider needs our help more than our criticism. Here is a brother who has fallen into sin, and we are prone to condemn and sit in judgment upon him. But we don't know all the circumstances which resulted in his falling. If we did, we might be far more gracious and patient. Notice that this brother was "overtaken" in a fault. That is quite a different thing than OVER-TAKING a sin. Some people go looking for sin, and go out of their way to find it. But this is not the case in our Scripture. This brother was "overtaken," implying that he was trying to get away from it, trying to avoid it, but because of weakness, failure of prayer, or failure to look to the Lord for victory, was overtaken. It was not deliberate sinning, but being "overcome" in a moment of weakness.

Such we are to restore, remembering our own weakness. If we were in this brother's shoes, we might have fallen even deeper. We do not know the battle he had, how much of a struggle he put up—but still went down. He may be a weak young Christian, still untaught in the Word. Let us not judge him, but help him instead. If we could know all the circumstances as God knows, we would be more kind and patient toward fallen, stumbling saints. Not in vain does I Corinthians 4:5 admonish us:

> Therefore judge nothing before the time, until the Lord come, who both will bring to light the hidden things of darkness, and will make manifest the counsels of the hearts: and then shall every man have praise of God (I Cor. 4:5).

Withhold your judgment of another till Jesus comes, and let Him be the judge. And why? Because He alone knows the secret of each heart, and sees the motives and efforts of even the seemingly most defeated Christian. He takes into consideration all the factors which affect our conduct, and all the circumstances of disposition and environment which make it easy or difficult to live a life of victory. We may condemn some stumbling, falling believer (even doubt his salvation), but be ignorant of the terrific battle he is having. That stumbling believer may be putting up a harder fight than some others who do not have to contend with the things this poor brother has to meet.

For Some It Is Easier

It is easier for some to live a life of victory than others, and this the Lord will take into consideration. It is easier to live an even, well-controlled life, if you have been born with a quiet, easy-going disposition, than if by your birth you received a fiery, trigger-finger temper, ready to pop off at the drop of the hat. Dispositions vary; there are Peters and there are Johns. We realize that this temper must be conquered and victory is possible, but it may mean a battle. Peter's old temper was still in evidence for some time after his conversion.

It is easier to live the Christian life in an office like the Radio Bible Class in an atmosphere of prayer and spiritual exercise, than for those of you who work in offices and shops for ungodly, cursing bosses, surrounded by smut, profanity and intemperance. The Lord will take all this into consideration. It is easier to live the Christian life with a sweet, consecrated, devoted wife, than to live it under the same roof with a carping, nagging, whining, fault-finding, worldly Xanthippe. Before judging your brother, remember this: God knows the peculiar weakness and temptations we have to face, and instead of condemning us, He assures us:

> There hath no temptation taken you but such as is common to man: but God is faithful, who will not suffer you to be tempted above that ye are able; but will with the temptation also make a way to escape, that ye may be able to bear it (I Cor. 10:13).

So remember, "brethren, if a man be overtaken in a fault, ye which are spiritual restore such an one in the spirit of meekness." "Ye who are spiritual, restore such an one." The evidence of spirituality is the willingness to be patient, kind, forbearing, forgiving toward the erring ones. Too often we have seen men who wanted to be known as spiritual, and put on a great show of piousness, with a long face, and longer prayers, who belied their spirituality by an intolerant, condemnatory, censorious, holier-than-thou attitude toward some weak, fallen brother or sister. Well do I remember one young couple who had fallen into sin, and came of their own accord to confess their sin before the official board of the church, only to be discouraged by the suggestion of a pious old deacon, that they should be put on probation for a few months to see if it was real. How foreign to Paul's words, "restore such an one in the spirit of meekness." The weaker the Christian, the more they need our welcome and encouragement. I think the Lord knew a whole lot more about the circumstances (which are not mentioned in the record) leading up to the sin of the adulterous woman brought by the Pharisees for His condemnation, but resulted in His encouraging words:

> Neither do I condemn thee: go, and sin no more (John 8:11).

Not long after the deacon's motion to place the ones

"overtaken in a fault" on probation, it came out that he was himself (not being overtaken) but chasing his pet sin with all his vigor. How fitting then the concluding phrase of the verse:

> . . . considering thyself, lest thou also be tempted (Gal. 6:1).

He that is without sin among you, cast the first stone. In Romans 14:1 we read:

> Him that is weak in the faith receive ye, but not to doubtful disputations (Rom. 14:1).

We are not to exclude the weaker believers or put them on probation, but receive them. The weaker they are the more they need our help and fellowship. In Romans 15:1 Paul says:

> We then that are strong ought to bear the infirmities of the weak (Rom. 15:1).

Oh, that God might teach us the lesson of self-judgment and self-condemnation, and that we would heed the words of I Corinthians 11:28.

LET A MAN EXAMINE HIMSELF

This admonition, therefore, on which we have dwelt at length is greatly needed. The reason for the "biting and devouring" of one another in Christian circles, the attitude toward weaker brethren, and those with whom we disagree, is a result of ignorance concerning the GRACE of God. It is an evidence of legality and carnality. The only cure for bigotry and fault-finding of others is to go back once more to the greatest exhibition of the grace of God—CALVARY! Behold there the spotless, perfect Son of God, nailed to a Cross, His back bruised and bleeding, a crown of thorns upon His head, His body covered with bloody sweat, His feet and hands nailed to the Cross, suffering the agonies of Hell for helpless, hopeless, Hell-deserving and Hell-bound sinners. Stand there and realize that it was for YOU that He hung there. You had no claim to His mercy, you had no right to His pardon, but it was all grace—grace—grace—undeserved and unmerited favor. Hear His cry, "My God, My God, why hast thou forsaken me?" And then consider that He was forsaken, that you might be accepted with all your guilt and shame. Can you then be proud, bigoted, unforgiving to others? It was all grace by which you were saved. Why then be so legal in your treatment of others?

Without rancor or bitterness, I want to say that the most intolerant, critical, condemnatory abusive people with whom we have to deal at the Radio Bible Class, the worst offenders are the champions of the LAW, who object to our preaching of grace. Of all the letters of abuse and condemnation we receive in the mail, the overwhelming majority are from those legalistic proselyters who would place us back under the law of commandments, and as in the days of the Colossians would judge us,

> . . . in meat, or in drink, or in respect of an holyday, or of the new moon, or of the sabbath days:
> Which are a shadow of things to come; but the body is of Christ (Col. 2:16, 17).

May our knowledge of His grace cause us to "stand fast," heeding the words of II Peter 3:17,

> . . . beware lest ye also, being led away with the error of the wicked, fall from your own stedfastness.
> But grow in grace, and in the knowledge of our Lord and Saviour Jesus Christ. To him be glory both now and for ever. Amen (II Pet. 3:17, 18).

Chapter Twenty-two

LIVING FOR CHRIST AND FOR OTHERS

> Bear ye one another's burdens, and so fulfil the law of Christ.
>
> For every man shall bear his own burden (Gal. 6:2, 5).

THE first verse of Galatians six is a solemn warning against legality and sitting in judgment upon weak, stumbling believers. It is a plea for compassion, forbearance and helpfulness to those who fall into sin. The sinner seeks sin—the believer flees sin. But even though he flees, he may still be "overtaken in a fault." Toward such we should be patient, kind and helpful, realizing the weaker the brother, the more he needs our sympathy and aid. Instead of condemning and avoiding him we are told to restore such an one in the spirit of meekness. The very opposite of a spirit of condemnation and censure against which we are indirectly warned in verse 1, is given in verse 2:

> Bear ye one another's burdens, and so fulfil the law of Christ (Gal. 6:2).

Instead of discouraging those who are weak and burdened, we are to "bear their burdens." And doing this, we fulfill the law of Christ, for love is the fulfilling of the law. A holier-than-thou attitude of criticism is the evidence of legality; forgiveness and forbearance are the evidences of grace. We are to bear one another's burdens.

177

But in verse 5 we seem to have a contradiction, for it says:

> For every man shall bear his own burden (Gal. 6:5).

Is this a contradiction? It would almost seem so until we point out that the word "burden" in verse 1, is not the same as the word in verse 5. In the verse, "Bear ye one another's burdens," the original is "baros" and the lexicon gives the meaning as "a heavy load or a weight." But in verse 5 the word is "phortion" and my concordance defines it as "a task or a service to be done." The weights or loads we are to help one another bear must be viewed in the light of the preceding verse (Gal. 6:1), where we are admonished to restore a weak brother overtaken in a fault. Instead of condemning such, and discouraging them, we are to assist them and help in overcoming the fault. We that are strong ought to bear the infirmities of the weak (Rom. 15:1). It includes instructing young believers, encouraging stumbling saints. It would include comforting the bereaved and afflicted, visiting the sick and lonely, assisting those who are in financial straits, counseling and advising in perplexities, guidance in the Word, and prayer for new converts. There are thousands of burdened souls whom we can help by prayer, encouragement, material assistance, and helpful counsel. How we can lift the burden of the forgotten souls in chronic sickness, in old age, and in poverty! This we believe to be the force of "bear ye one another's burdens, and so fulfil the law of Christ." This burden-bearing is not a legal obligation, but it goes far beyond the demands of the law. It is motivated by grace and love, and is the obedience to the new law of liberty. It is keeping His commandments.

And this is his commandment, That we should believe

on the name of his Son Jesus Christ, and LOVE ONE ANOTHER, as he gave us commandment (I John 3:23).

THE PERSONAL BURDEN

These then are the burdens we can share with others. But there are other burdens which are personal, not to be shared by any other. The statement is clear:

> For every man shall bear his own burden (Gal. 6:5).

Again the first word of this verse, FOR, refers us back to the context for its interpretation. After the statement, "bear ye one another's burdens," we read:

> For if a man think himself to be something, when he is nothing, he deceiveth himself (Gal. 6:3).

We are to be willing to stoop to another's needs, and go out of our way to be of assistance. If we feel we are too important to deal with a weaker brother or a poorer sister or a needy neighbor, we are only deceiving ourselves and no one else, for it reveals a lack of grace and love within the heart. Uppishness and snobbery have no place in a life which is filled with grace. Early in my ministry I had a few rather wealthy people in my congregation who belonged to the "upper crust." During our ministry a father and mother were converted, and began to attend the services. They were very poor, having had no end of sickness and hospital expenses. They drove an old dilapidated Ford, and their clothes though clean were patch upon patch. Some of my uppish members rather resented their presence and openly showed their disapproval. When I came to the defense of this poor family and tried to explain their circumstances, one family just up and left, soon to be followed by others. Yet anyone of these could have helped to bear the burden. They could have relieved their poverty, bought all of

them new clothes and a car beside, and never have missed
the cost, but they preferred not to bear one another's
burdens. How we do need the counsel of I John 3:16, 17.

> Hereby perceive we the love of God, because he laid
> down his life for us: and we ought to lay down our lives
> for the brethren.
>
> But whoso hath this world's good, and seeth his brother
> have need, and shutteth up his bowels of compassion from
> him, how dwelleth the love of God in him? (I John 3:16, 17).

To all such we repeat, "For if a man think himself to
be something, when he is nothing, he deceiveth himself."
The next verse begins with a BUT. It introduces a contrast between the burdens of verse 2 and the burden of
verse 5:

> But let every man prove his own WORK, and then shall
> he have rejoicing in himself alone, and not in another.
> FOR EVERY MAN SHALL BEAR HIS OWN BURDEN
> (Gal. 6:4, 5).

He is speaking here of WORK, personal work, a personal task which no one else can do for him. It is his
own personal responsibility. The word "burden" is the
same as the word used in Matthew 11:30. Jesus in this
verse is talking about service. The invitation of Matthew
11:28 is to sinners:

> Come unto me, all ye that labour and are heavy laden
> (Matt. 11:28).

This is Christ's invitation to the unsaved to come and
receive the free gift of life. But in the next verse we have
an invitation, NOT to the sinner, but to the SAINT. It
is Christ's call to those who have already come to Him
for salvation, to now come AFTER Him for service. It
deals with a yoke, the symbol of toil, service and work.

> Take my yoke upon you, and learn of me.... (Matt.
> 11:29).

It is then that Jesus says:

> For my yoke is easy, and my BURDEN is light (Matt.
> 11:30).

The burden here is associated with the yoke of service, obedience and submission. Now the word "burden" in Galatians 6:5 is the same word as in Matthew 11:30. It refers to personal discipleship and service. And of this Paul says no one else can substitute for you. It is your own individual personal responsibility for service. Each one of us has a job to do which we only can do. All of us have our own talents, gifts and opportunities. If we fail in our personal faithfulness, no one else can help bear the burden, for it is ours alone. This is the meaning of "Every man shall bear his own burden." As the preceding verse indicates, it has to do with WORK.

> Let every man (individually) prove his own work.

May we by God's grace not only learn to bear one another's burdens, but not to neglect our own personal responsibilities.

> Having then gifts differing according to the grace that is given to us, whether prophecy, let us prophesy according to the proportion of faith;
> Or ministry, let us wait on our ministering: or he that teacheth, on teaching;
> Or he that exhorteth, on exhortation: he that giveth, let him do it with simplicity; he that ruleth, with diligence; he that sheweth mercy, with cheerfulness (Rom. 12:6-8).

There is a personal job God has given to each one, which no one else can do for us.

SOWING AND REAPING

In Galatians 6, verse 6, an example of personal responsibility is given:

> Let him that is taught in the word communicate unto him that teacheth in all good things (Gal. 6:6).

Those who preach the gospel shall live by the gospel, and those who minister in spiritual things should be relieved of temporal cares by the generosity of those taught in the Word. And then follows a note of warning that we are to give an account of our burden-bearing and service:

> Be not deceived; God is not mocked: for whatsoever a man soweth, that shall he also reap.
> For he that soweth to his flesh shall of the flesh reap corruption; but he that soweth to the Spirit shall of the Spirit reap life everlasting (Gal. 6:7, 8).

We are reminded that there is a time of reckoning coming and we shall receive our rewards on the basis of our faithfulness. The Lord will consider our handicaps, our obstacles, our peculiar burdens, as well as our motives and talents and opportunities, and so the assurance:

> And let us not be weary in well doing: for in due season we shall reap, if we faint not.
> As we have therefore opportunity, let us do good unto all men, especially unto them who are of the household of faith (Gal. 6:9, 10).

We come now to the conclusion of the letter. Paul calls their attention to the fact that he personally had written this letter instead of dictating it to an amanuensis:

> Ye see how large a letter I have written unto you with mine own hand (Gal. 6:11).

Apparently most of Paul's letters were dictated to another. It is thought this was because of Paul's weak eyes with which he was afflicted. But the situation in Galatia called for such urgency that he did not wait for his secretary, but wrote the letter in a large bold scrawl. The expression, "Ye see how large a letter I have written," should be, "Ye see with what big letters I have written."

Before closing, Paul issues a final warning against being deceived by the false teachers of the law. He says:

> As many as desire to make a fair shew in the flesh, they constrain you to be circumcised; only lest they should suffer persecution for the cross of Christ.
>
> For neither they themselves who are circumcised keep the law; but desire to have you circumcised, that they may glory in your flesh (Gal. 6:12, 13).

The epistle closes with an affirmation by Paul concerning his determination never to waver from the preaching of his message of grace. He will not go back to Sinai after having been at Calvary. He will not go back to the law after having tasted the grace of God. Listen to the testimony.

THREE CRUCIFIXIONS

> But God forbid that I should glory, save in the cross of our Lord Jesus Christ, by whom the world is crucified unto me, and I unto the world (Gal. 6:14).

Paul wraps up his argument with a picture of three crucifixions in this verse:

1. The crucifixion of Christ—the basis.
2. The crucifixion of the world—the result.
3. The crucifixion of self—the victory.

Our salvation rests on the crucifixion of Christ. Our position resting on this foundation is guaranteed by the world being crucified to us, and victory comes when we are crucified unto the world. The Cross is the place of death. By the Cross of Christ, we are reckoned to be dead:

1. To the law.
2. To the world.
3. To self.

But those who died in Christ are also raised with Christ, and live in the newness of life. Paul ends the epistle with:

> And as many as walk according to this rule, peace be on them, and mercy, and upon the Israel of God.
> From henceforth let no man trouble me: for I bear in my body the marks of the Lord Jesus.
> Brethren, the grace of our Lord Jesus Christ be with your spirit. Amen (Gal. 6:16-18).

The epistle ends with GRACE (Gal. 6:18) as it opened with GRACE (Gal. 1:3).

BY THE GRACE OF GOD
DEAD TO THE LAW—ALIVE UNTO GOD